ALSO BY SEAMUS HEANEY

POETRY

Death of a Naturalist

Door into the Dark

Wintering Out

North

Field Work

Selected Poems 1965–1975

Station Island

Sweeney Astray

Sweeney's Flight
(with photographs by
Rachel Giese)

The Haw Lantern

*New Selected Poems
1966–1987*

Seeing Things

Laments by Jan
Kochanowski (translated
with Stanisław Barańczak)

The Spirit Level

*Opened Ground:
Selected Poems 1966–1996*

Beowulf

Electric Light

District and Circle

*The Testament of
Cresseid & Seven Fables*

Human Chain

Selected Poems 1966–1987

Selected Poems 1988–2013

Aeneid Book VI

AS EDITOR

The Rattle Bag
(with Ted Hughes)

The School Bag
(with Ted Hughes)

PROSE

*Preoccupations: Selected
Prose 1968–1978*

*The Government
of the Tongue*

*The Redress of Poetry:
Oxford Lectures*

*Finders Keepers:
Selected Prose 1971–2001*

Stepping Stones
(with Dennis O'Driscoll)

PLAYS

The Cure at Troy

The Burial at Thebes

100 Poems

100 Poems

Seamus Heaney

Farrar, Straus and Giroux   New York

Farrar, Straus and Giroux
120 Broadway, New York 10271

Printed in the United States of America
Originally published in 2018 by Faber & Faber Ltd, Great Britain
Published in the United States by Farrar, Straus and Giroux
First American edition, 2019

Library of Congress Cataloging-in-Publication Data
Names: Heaney, Seamus, author.
Title: 100 poems / Seamus Heaney.
Other titles: One hundred poems
Description: New York : Farrar, Straus and Giroux, 2019. |
    Includes index.
Identifiers: LCCN 2019000365 | ISBN 9780374100292 (hardcover)
Classification: LCC PR6058.E2 A6 2019 | DDC 821/.914—dc23
LC record available at https://lccn.loc.gov/2019000365

Our books may be purchased in bulk for promotional, educational,
or business use. Please contact your local bookseller or the Macmillan
Corporate and Premium Sales Department at 1-800-221-7945, extension
5442, or by e-mail at MacmillanSpecialMarkets@macmillan.com.

www.fsgbooks.com
www.twitter.com/fsgbooks • www.facebook.com/fsgbooks

1 3 5 7 9 10 8 6 4 2

Contents

Family Note

The idea for this collection of one hundred poems is not a new one. My father himself had contemplated such a book, particularly in later years, and had gone as far as discussing it with his editor and close confidants. The notion of a 'trim' selection appealed to him, and while he had chosen and edited *Selected Poems 1965–1975*, *New Selected Poems 1966–1987* and *Opened Ground: Selected Poems 1966–1996* – as well as many editions in translation – no single volume existed representing the entire sweep of his career, from first collection to last.

Now, almost five years after his death, we, his immediate family, have returned to that idea. By its very nature, this is a different selection from the one Dad might have made – or an independent editor, for that matter. We took the decision to draw from the twelve original collections (with two exceptions) and leave aside his translations of *Sweeney Astray*, *Beowulf* and others. It includes many of his best-loved and most celebrated poems, as well as others that were among his favourites to read and which conjure up that much-missed voice. However, we also made some choices that have special resonance for us individually: evocations of departed friends; remembered moments from a long-ago holiday; familiar objects from our family home. Each one of us – my mother, Marie, my brothers, Michael and Christopher, and I – approached the task with a lifetime's memories, no one more so than my mother, who had to choose from a trove of love poems spanning fifty years. Perhaps inevitably, the resulting selection is imbued with personal recollections of our shared lives.

Yet we hope that everyone will find something here to cherish or be surprised by: that a newcomer will enjoy reading these poems for the first time, and that the long-time devotee might rediscover a forgotten favourite or simply listen again to the poetic voice as it changes and matures over the course of the years. Indeed, many readers will come to this book with their own particular memories and associations – of times when a poem helped to mark a moment of joy, perhaps, or offered consolation.

Finally, rather than being an 'in memoriam' volume, this collection is intended as a celebration of the extraordinary person who gave us these poems. He himself once said that he had begun to think of life as 'a series of ripples widening out from an original centre'; we hope this book serves as a reminder of the power and vitality of his work, and a testament to its continuing life, rippling outwards with every new reader.

CATHERINE HEANEY

100 Poems

Digging

Between my finger and my thumb
The squat pen rests; snug as a gun.

Under my window, a clean rasping sound
When the spade sinks into gravelly ground:
My father, digging. I look down

Till his straining rump among the flowerbeds
Bends low, comes up twenty years away
Stooping in rhythm through potato drills
Where he was digging.

The coarse boot nestled on the lug, the shaft
Against the inside knee was levered firmly.
He rooted out tall tops, buried the bright edge deep
To scatter new potatoes that we picked
Loving their cool hardness in our hands.

By God, the old man could handle a spade.
Just like his old man.

My grandfather cut more turf in a day
Than any other man on Toner's bog.
Once I carried him milk in a bottle
Corked sloppily with paper. He straightened up
To drink it, then fell to right away
Nicking and slicing neatly, heaving sods
Over his shoulder, going down and down
For the good turf. Digging.

The cold smell of potato mould, the squelch and slap
Of soggy peat, the curt cuts of an edge
Through living roots awaken in my head.
But I've no spade to follow men like them.

Between my finger and my thumb
The squat pen rests.
I'll dig with it.

Death of a Naturalist

All year the flax-dam festered in the heart
Of the townland; green and heavy-headed
Flax had rotted there, weighted down by huge sods.
Daily it sweltered in the punishing sun.
Bubbles gargled delicately, bluebottles
Wove a strong gauze of sound around the smell.
There were dragonflies, spotted butterflies,
But best of all was the warm thick slobber
Of frogspawn that grew like clotted water
In the shade of the banks. Here, every spring
I would fill jampotfuls of the jellied
Specks to range on window-sills at home,
On shelves at school, and wait and watch until
The fattening dots burst into nimble-
Swimming tadpoles. Miss Walls would tell us how
The daddy frog was called a bullfrog
And how he croaked and how the mammy frog
Laid hundreds of little eggs and this was
Frogspawn. You could tell the weather by frogs too
For they were yellow in the sun and brown
In rain.

Then one hot day when fields were rank
With cowdung in the grass the angry frogs
Invaded the flax-dam; I ducked through hedges
To a coarse croaking that I had not heard
Before. The air was thick with a bass chorus.
Right down the dam gross-bellied frogs were cocked

On sods; their loose necks pulsed like sails. Some hopped:
The slap and plop were obscene threats. Some sat
Poised like mud grenades, their blunt heads farting.
I sickened, turned, and ran. The great slime kings
Were gathered there for vengeance and I knew
That if I dipped my hand the spawn would clutch it.

Blackberry-Picking

for Philip Hobsbaum

Late August, given heavy rain and sun
For a full week, the blackberries would ripen.
At first, just one, a glossy purple clot
Among others, red, green, hard as a knot.
You ate that first one and its flesh was sweet
Like thickened wine: summer's blood was in it
Leaving stains upon the tongue and lust for
Picking. Then red ones inked up and that hunger
Sent us out with milk cans, pea tins, jam pots
Where briars scratched and wet grass bleached our boots.
Round hayfields, cornfields and potato drills
We trekked and picked until the cans were full,
Until the tinkling bottom had been covered
With green ones, and on top big dark blobs burned
Like a plate of eyes. Our hands were peppered
With thorn pricks, our palms sticky as Bluebeard's.

We hoarded the fresh berries in the byre.
But when the bath was filled we found a fur,
A rat-grey fungus, glutting on our cache.
The juice was stinking too. Once off the bush
The fruit fermented, the sweet flesh would turn sour.
I always felt like crying. It wasn't fair
That all the lovely canfuls smelt of rot.
Each year I hoped they'd keep, knew they would not.

Follower

My father worked with a horse-plough,
His shoulders globed like a full sail strung
Between the shafts and the furrow.
The horses strained at his clicking tongue.

An expert. He would set the wing
And fit the bright steel-pointed sock.
The sod rolled over without breaking.
At the headrig, with a single pluck

Of reins, the sweating team turned round
And back into the land. His eye
Narrowed and angled at the ground,
Mapping the furrow exactly.

I stumbled in his hobnailed wake,
Fell sometimes on the polished sod;
Sometimes he rode me on his back
Dipping and rising to his plod.

I wanted to grow up and plough,
To close one eye, stiffen my arm.
All I ever did was follow
In his broad shadow round the farm.

I was a nuisance, tripping, falling,
Yapping always. But today
It is my father who keeps stumbling
Behind me, and will not go away.

Mid-Term Break

I sat all morning in the college sick bay
Counting bells knelling classes to a close.
At two o'clock our neighbours drove me home.

In the porch I met my father crying –
He had always taken funerals in his stride –
And Big Jim Evans saying it was a hard blow.

The baby cooed and laughed and rocked the pram
When I came in, and I was embarrassed
By old men standing up to shake my hand

And tell me they were 'sorry for my trouble'.
Whispers informed strangers I was the eldest,
Away at school, as my mother held my hand

In hers and coughed out angry tearless sighs.
At ten o'clock the ambulance arrived
With the corpse, stanched and bandaged by the nurses.

Next morning I went up into the room. Snowdrops
And candles soothed the bedside; I saw him
For the first time in six weeks. Paler now,

Wearing a poppy bruise on his left temple,
He lay in the four-foot box as in his cot.
No gaudy scars, the bumper knocked him clear.

A four-foot box, a foot for every year.

The Diviner

Cut from the green hedge a forked hazel stick
That he held tight by the arms of the V:
Circling the terrain, hunting the pluck
Of water, nervous, but professionally

Unfussed. The pluck came sharp as a sting.
The rod jerked with precise convulsions,
Spring water suddenly broadcasting
Through a green hazel its secret stations.

The bystanders would ask to have a try.
He handed them the rod without a word.
It lay dead in their grasp till, nonchalantly,
He gripped expectant wrists. The hazel stirred.

Twice Shy

Her scarf *à la* Bardot,
In suede flats for the walk,
She came with me one evening
For air and friendly talk.
We crossed the quiet river,
Took the embankment walk.

Traffic holding its breath,
Sky a tense diaphragm:
Dusk hung like a backcloth
That shook where a swan swam,
Tremulous as a hawk
Hanging deadly, calm.

A vacuum of need
Collapsed each hunting heart
But tremulously we held
As hawk and prey apart,
Preserved classic decorum,
Deployed our talk with art.

Our juvenilia
Had taught us both to wait,
Not to publish feeling
And regret it all too late –
Mushroom loves already
Had puffed and burst in hate.

So, chary and excited
As a thrush linked on a hawk,
We thrilled to the March twilight
With nervous childish talk:
Still waters running deep
Along the embankment walk.

Scaffolding

Masons, when they start upon a building,
Are careful to test out the scaffolding;

Make sure that planks won't slip at busy points,
Secure all ladders, tighten bolted joints.

And yet all this comes down when the job's done,
Showing off walls of sure and solid stone.

So if, my dear, there sometimes seem to be
Old bridges breaking between you and me,

Never fear. We may let the scaffolds fall,
Confident that we have built our wall.

Personal Helicon

for Michael Longley

As a child, they could not keep me from wells
And old pumps with buckets and windlasses.
I loved the dark drop, the trapped sky, the smells
Of waterweed, fungus and dank moss.

One, in a brickyard, with a rotted board top.
I savoured the rich crash when a bucket
Plummeted down at the end of a rope.
So deep you saw no reflection in it.

A shallow one under a dry stone ditch
Fructified like any aquarium.
When you dragged out long roots from the soft mulch
A white face hovered over the bottom.

Others had echoes, gave back your own call
With a clean new music in it. And one
Was scaresome, for there, out of ferns and tall
Foxgloves, a rat slapped across my reflection.

Now, to pry into roots, to finger slime,
To stare, big-eyed Narcissus, into some spring
Is beneath all adult dignity. I rhyme
To see myself, to set the darkness echoing.

The Forge

All I know is a door into the dark.
Outside, old axles and iron hoops rusting;
Inside, the hammered anvil's short-pitched ring,
The unpredictable fantail of sparks
Or hiss when a new shoe toughens in water.
The anvil must be somewhere in the centre,
Horned as a unicorn, at one end square,
Set there immoveable: an altar
Where he expends himself in shape and music.
Sometimes, leather-aproned, hairs in his nose,
He leans out on the jamb, recalls a clatter
Of hoofs where traffic is flashing in rows;
Then grunts and goes in, with a slam and flick
To beat real iron out, to work the bellows.

The Peninsula

When you have nothing more to say, just drive
For a day all round the peninsula.
The sky is tall as over a runway,
The land without marks, so you will not arrive

But pass through, though always skirting landfall.
At dusk, horizons drink down sea and hill,
The ploughed field swallows the whitewashed gable
And you're in the dark again. Now recall

The glazed foreshore and silhouetted log,
That rock where breakers shredded into rags,
The leggy birds stilted on their own legs,
Islands riding themselves out into the fog,

And drive back home, still with nothing to say
Except that now you will uncode all landscapes
By this: things founded clean on their own shapes,
Water and ground in their extremity.

Requiem for the Croppies

The pockets of our greatcoats full of barley –
No kitchens on the run, no striking camp –
We moved quick and sudden in our own country.
The priest lay behind ditches with the tramp.
A people, hardly marching – on the hike –
We found new tactics happening each day:
We'd cut through reins and rider with the pike
And stampede cattle into infantry,
Then retreat through hedges where cavalry must be thrown.
Until, on Vinegar Hill, the fatal conclave.
Terraced thousands died, shaking scythes at cannon.
The hillside blushed, soaked in our broken wave.
They buried us without shroud or coffin
And in August the barley grew up out of the grave.

Night Drive

The smells of ordinariness
Were new on the night drive through France:
Rain and hay and woods on the air
Made warm draughts in the open car.

Signposts whitened relentlessly.
Montreuil, Abbeville, Beauvais
Were promised, promised, came and went,
Each place granting its name's fulfilment.

A combine groaning its way late
Bled seeds across its work-light.
A forest fire smouldered out.
One by one small cafés shut.

I thought of you continuously
A thousand miles south where Italy
Laid its loin to France on the darkened sphere.
Your ordinariness was renewed there.

The Given Note

On the most westerly Blasket
In a dry-stone hut
He got this air out of the night.

Strange noises were heard
By others who followed, bits of a tune
Coming in on loud weather

Though nothing like melody.
He blamed their fingers and ear
As unpractised, their fiddling easy

For he had gone alone into the island
And brought back the whole thing.
The house throbbed like his full violin.

So whether he calls it spirit music
Or not, I don't care. He took it
Out of wind off mid-Atlantic.

Still he maintains, from nowhere.
It comes off the bow gravely,
Rephrases itself into the air.

Bogland

for T. P. Flanagan

We have no prairies
To slice a big sun at evening –
Everywhere the eye concedes to
Encroaching horizon,

Is wooed into the cyclops' eye
Of a tarn. Our unfenced country
Is bog that keeps crusting
Between the sights of the sun.

They've taken the skeleton
Of the Great Irish Elk
Out of the peat, set it up,
An astounding crate full of air.

Butter sunk under
More than a hundred years
Was recovered salty and white.
The ground itself is kind, black butter

Melting and opening underfoot,
Missing its last definition
By millions of years.
They'll never dig coal here,

Only the waterlogged trunks
Of great firs, soft as pulp.
Our pioneers keep striking
Inwards and downwards,

Every layer they strip
Seems camped on before.
The bogholes might be Atlantic seepage.
The wet centre is bottomless.

Anahorish

My 'place of clear water',
the first hill in the world
where springs washed into
the shiny grass

and darkened cobbles
in the bed of the lane.
Anahorish, soft gradient
of consonant, vowel-meadow,

after-image of lamps
swung through the yards
on winter evenings.
With pails and barrows

those mound-dwellers
go waist-deep in mist
to break the light ice
at wells and dunghills.

Broagh

Riverbank, the long rigs
ending in broad docken
and a canopied pad
down to the ford.

The garden mould
bruised easily, the shower
gathering in your heelmark
was the black *O*

in *Broagh*,
its low tattoo
among the windy boortrees
and rhubarb-blades

ended almost
suddenly, like that last
gh the strangers found
difficult to manage.

The Other Side

Thigh-deep in sedge and marigolds,
a neighbour laid his shadow
on the stream, vouching

'It's as poor as Lazarus, that ground,'
and brushed away
among the shaken leafage.

I lay where his lea sloped
to meet our fallow,
nested on moss and rushes,

my ear swallowing
his fabulous, biblical dismissal,
that tongue of chosen people.

When he would stand like that
on the other side, white-haired,
swinging his blackthorn

at the marsh weeds,
he prophesied above our scraggy acres,
then turned away

towards his promised furrows
on the hill, a wake of pollen
drifting to our bank, next season's tares.

II

For days we would rehearse
each patriarchal dictum:
Lazarus, the Pharaoh, Solomon

and David and Goliath rolled
magnificently, like loads of hay
too big for our small lanes,

or faltered on a rut –
'Your side of the house, I believe,
hardly rule by the Book at all.'

His brain was a whitewashed kitchen
hung with texts, swept tidy
as the body o' the kirk.

III

Then sometimes when the rosary was dragging
mournfully on in the kitchen
we would hear his step round the gable

though not until after the litany
would the knock come to the door
and the casual whistle strike up

on the doorstep. 'A right-looking night,'
he might say, 'I was dandering by
and says I, I might as well call.'

But now I stand behind him
in the dark yard, in the moan of prayers.
He puts a hand in a pocket

or taps a little tune with the blackthorn
shyly, as if he were party to
lovemaking or a stranger's weeping.

Should I slip away, I wonder,
or go up and touch his shoulder
and talk about the weather

or the price of grass-seed?

The Tollund Man

Some day I will go to Aarhus
To see his peat-brown head,
The mild pods of his eyelids,
His pointed skin cap.

In the flat country nearby
Where they dug him out,
His last gruel of winter seeds
Caked in his stomach,

Naked except for
The cap, noose and girdle,
I will stand a long time.
Bridegroom to the goddess,

She tightened her torc on him
And opened her fen,
Those dark juices working
Him to a saint's kept body,

Trove of the turfcutters'
Honeycombed workings.
Now his stained face
Reposes at Aarhus.

II

I could risk blasphemy,
Consecrate the cauldron bog
Our holy ground and pray
Him to make germinate

The scattered, ambushed
Flesh of labourers,
Stockinged corpses
Laid out in the farmyards,

Tell-tale skin and teeth
Flecking the sleepers
Of four young brothers, trailed
For miles along the lines.

III

Something of his sad freedom
As he rode the tumbril
Should come to me, driving,
Saying the names

Tollund, Grauballe, Nebelgard,
Watching the pointing hands
Of country people,
Not knowing their tongue.

Out there in Jutland
In the old man-killing parishes
I will feel lost,
Unhappy and at home.

Wedding Day

I am afraid.
Sound has stopped in the day
And the images reel over
And over. Why all those tears,

The wild grief on his face
Outside the taxi? The sap
Of mourning rises
In our waving guests.

You sing behind the tall cake
Like a deserted bride
Who persists, demented,
And goes through the ritual.

When I went to the Gents
There was a skewered heart
And a legend of love. Let me
Sleep on your breast to the airport.

Westering

in California

I sit under Rand McNally's
'Official Map of the Moon' –
The colour of frogskin,
Its enlarged pores held

Open and one called
'Pitiscus' at eye level –
Recalling the last night
In Donegal, my shadow

Neat upon the whitewash
From her bony shine,
The cobbles of the yard
Lit pale as eggs.

Summer had been a free fall
Ending there,
The empty amphitheatre
Of the west. Good Friday

We had started out
Past shopblinds drawn on the afternoon,
Cars stilled outside still churches,
Bikes tilting to a wall;

We drove by,
A dwindling interruption,
As clappers smacked
On a bare altar

And congregations bent
To the studded crucifix.
What nails dropped out that hour?
Roads unreeled, unreeled

Falling light as casts
Laid down
On shining waters.
Under the moon's stigmata

Six thousand miles away,
I imagine untroubled dust,
A loosening gravity,
Christ weighing by his hands.

Mossbawn: Two Poems in Dedication

for Mary Heaney

1 *Sunlight*

There was a sunlit absence.
The helmeted pump in the yard
heated its iron,
water honeyed

in the slung bucket
and the sun stood
like a griddle cooling
against the wall

of each long afternoon.
So, her hands scuffled
over the bakeboard,
the reddening stove

sent its plaque of heat
against her where she stood
in a floury apron
by the window.

Now she dusts the board
with a goose's wing,
now sits, broad-lapped,
with whitened nails

and measling shins:
here is a space
again, the scone rising
to the tick of two clocks.

And here is love
like a tinsmith's scoop
sunk past its gleam
in the meal-bin.

2 *The Seed Cutters*

They seem hundreds of years away. Brueghel,
You'll know them if I can get them true.
They kneel under the hedge in a half-circle
Behind a windbreak wind is breaking through.
They are the seed cutters. The tuck and frill
Of leaf-sprout is on the seed potatoes
Buried under that straw. With time to kill,
They are taking their time. Each sharp knife goes
Lazily halving each root that falls apart
In the palm of the hand: a milky gleam,
And, at the centre, a dark watermark.
Oh, calendar customs! Under the broom
Yellowing over them, compose the frieze
With all of us there, our anonymities.

Funeral Rites

I shouldered a kind of manhood
stepping in to lift the coffins
of dead relations.
They had been laid out

in tainted rooms,
their eyelids glistening,
their dough-white hands
shackled in rosary beads.

Their puffed knuckles
had unwrinkled, the nails
were darkened, the wrists
obediently sloped.

The dulse-brown shroud,
the quilted satin cribs:
I knelt courteously
admiring it all

as wax melted down
and veined the candles,
the flames hovering
to the women hovering

behind me.
And always, in a corner,
the coffin lid,
its nail-heads dressed

with little gleaming crosses.
Dear soapstone masks,
kissing their igloo brows
had to suffice

before the nails were sunk
and the black glacier
of each funeral
pushed away.

II

Now as news comes in
of each neighbourly murder
we pine for ceremony,
customary rhythms:

the temperate footsteps
of a cortège, winding past
each blinded home.
I would restore

the great chambers of Boyne,
prepare a sepulchre
under the cupmarked stones.
Out of side-streets and by-roads

purring family cars
nose into line,
the whole country tunes
to the muffled drumming

of ten thousand engines.
Somnambulant women,
left behind, move
through emptied kitchens

imagining our slow triumph
towards the mounds.
Quiet as a serpent
in its grassy boulevard,

the procession drags its tail
out of the Gap of the North
as its head already enters
the megalithic doorway.

III

When they have put the stone
back in its mouth
we will drive north again
past Strang and Carling fjords,

the cud of memory
allayed for once, arbitration
of the feud placated,
imagining those under the hill

disposed like Gunnar
who lay beautiful
inside his burial mound,
though dead by violence

and unavenged.
Men said that he was chanting
verses about honour
and that four lights burned

in corners of the chamber:
which opened then, as he turned
with a joyful face
to look at the moon.

The Grauballe Man

As if he had been poured
in tar, he lies
on a pillow of turf
and seems to weep

the black river of himself.
The grain of his wrists
is like bog oak,
the ball of his heel

like a basalt egg.
His instep has shrunk
cold as a swan's foot
or a wet swamp root.

His hips are the ridge
and purse of a mussel,
his spine an eel arrested
under a glisten of mud.

The head lifts,
the chin is a visor
raised above the vent
of his slashed throat

that has tanned and toughened.
The cured wound
opens inwards to a dark
elderberry place.

Who will say 'corpse'
to his vivid cast?
Who will say 'body'
to his opaque repose?

And his rusted hair,
a mat unlikely
as a foetus's.
I first saw his twisted face

in a photograph,
a head and shoulder
out of the peat,
bruised like a forceps baby,

but now he lies
perfected in my memory,
down to the red horn
of his nails,

hung in the scales
with beauty and atrocity:
with the Dying Gaul
too strictly compassed

on his shield,
with the actual weight
of each hooded victim,
slashed and dumped.

Punishment

I can feel the tug
of the halter at the nape
of her neck, the wind
on her naked front.

It blows her nipples
to amber beads,
it shakes the frail rigging
of her ribs.

I can see her drowned
body in the bog,
the weighing stone,
the floating rods and boughs.

Under which at first
she was a barked sapling
that is dug up
oak-bone, brain-firkin:

her shaved head
like a stubble of black corn,
her blindfold a soiled bandage,
her noose a ring

to store
the memories of love.
Little adulteress,
before they punished you

you were flaxen-haired,
undernourished, and your
tar-black face was beautiful.
My poor scapegoat,

I almost love you
but would have cast, I know,
the stones of silence.
I am the artful voyeur

of your brain's exposed
and darkened combs,
your muscles' webbing
and all your numbered bones:

I who have stood dumb
when your betraying sisters,
cauled in tar,
wept by the railings,

who would connive
in civilized outrage
yet understand the exact
and tribal, intimate revenge.

from Whatever You Say Say Nothing

I

I'm writing this just after an encounter
With an English journalist in search of 'views
On the Irish thing'. I'm back in winter
Quarters where bad news is no longer news,

Where media-men and stringers sniff and point,
Where zoom lenses, recorders and coiled leads
Litter the hotels. The times are out of joint
But I incline as much to rosary beads

As to the jottings and analyses
Of politicians and newspapermen
Who've scribbled down the long campaign from gas
And protest to gelignite and Sten,

Who proved upon their pulses 'escalate',
'Backlash' and 'crack down', 'the provisional wing',
'Polarization' and 'long-standing hate'.
Yet I live here, I live here too, I sing,

Expertly civil-tongued with civil neighbours
On the high wires of first wireless reports,
Sucking the fake taste, the stony flavours
Of those sanctioned, old, elaborate retorts:

'Oh, it's disgraceful, surely, I agree.'
'Where's it going to end?' 'It's getting worse.'
'They're murderers.' 'Internment, understandably . . .'
The 'voice of sanity' is getting hoarse.

'Religion's never mentioned here,' of course.
'You know them by their eyes,' and hold your tongue.
'One side's as bad as the other,' never worse.
Christ, it's near time that some small leak was sprung

In the great dykes the Dutchman made
To dam the dangerous tide that followed Seamus.
Yet for all this art and sedentary trade
I am incapable. The famous

Northern reticence, the tight gag of place
And times: yes, yes. Of the 'wee six' I sing
Where to be saved you only must save face
And whatever you say, you say nothing.

Smoke-signals are loud-mouthed compared with us:
Manoeuvrings to find out name and school,
Subtle discrimination by addresses
With hardly an exception to the rule

That Norman, Ken and Sidney signalled Prod
And Seamus (call me Sean) was sure-fire Pape.
O land of password, handgrip, wink and nod,
Of open minds as open as a trap,

Where tongues lie coiled, as under flames lie wicks,
Where half of us, as in a wooden horse,
Were cabin'd and confined like wily Greeks,
Besieged within the siege, whispering morse.

IV

This morning from a dewy motorway
I saw the new camp for the internees:
A bomb had left a crater of fresh clay
In the roadside, and over in the trees

Machine-gun posts defined a real stockade.
There was that white mist you get on a low ground
And it was déjà-vu, some film made
Of Stalag 17, a bad dream with no sound.

Is there a life before death? That's chalked up
In Ballymurphy. Competence with pain,
Coherent miseries, a bite and sup:
We hug our little destiny again.

from Singing School

1 *The Ministry of Fear*
for Seamus Deane

Well, as Kavanagh said, we have lived
In important places. The lonely scarp
Of St Columb's College, where I billeted
For six years, overlooked your Bogside.
I gazed into new worlds: the inflamed throat
Of Brandywell, its floodlit dogtrack,
The throttle of the hare. In the first week
I was so homesick I couldn't even eat
The biscuits left to sweeten my exile.
I threw them over the fence one night
In September 1951
When the lights of houses in the Lecky Road
Were amber in the fog. It was an act
Of stealth.
             Then Belfast, and then Berkeley.
Here's two on's are sophisticated,
Dabbling in verses till they have become
A life: from bulky envelopes arriving
In vacation time to slim volumes
Despatched 'with the author's compliments'.
Those poems in longhand, ripped from the wire spine
Of your exercise book, bewildered me –
Vowels and ideas bandied free
As the seed-pods blowing off our sycamores.
I tried to write about the sycamores
And innovated a South Derry rhyme

With *hushed* and *lulled* full chimes for *pushed*
    and *pulled*.
Those hobnailed boots from beyond the mountain
Were walking, by God, all over the fine
Lawns of elocution.
                            Have our accents
Changed? 'Catholics, in general, don't speak
As well as students from the Protestant schools.'
Remember that stuff? Inferiority
Complexes, stuff that dreams were made on.
'What's your name, Heaney?'
                                    'Heaney, Father.'
                                                    'Fair

Enough.'
            On my first day, the leather strap
Went epileptic in the Big Study,
Its echoes plashing over our bowed heads,
But I still wrote home that a boarder's life
Was not so bad, shying as usual.

On long vacations, then, I came to life
In the kissing seat of an Austin 16
Parked at a gable, the engine running,
My fingers tight as ivy on her shoulders,
A light left burning for her in the kitchen.
And heading back for home, the summer's
Freedom dwindling night by night, the air
All moonlight and a scent of hay, policemen
Swung their crimson flashlamps, crowding round
The car like black cattle, snuffing and pointing
The muzzle of a Sten gun in my eye:
'What's your name, driver?'
                                    'Seamus . . .'
                                            Seamus?

They once read my letters at a roadblock
And shone their torches on your hieroglyphics,
'Svelte dictions' in a very florid hand.

Ulster was British, but with no rights on
The English lyric: all around us, though
We hadn't named it, the ministry of fear.

2 *A Constable Calls*

His bicycle stood at the window-sill,
The rubber cowl of a mud-splasher
Skirting the front mudguard,
Its fat black handlegrips

Heating in sunlight, the 'spud'
Of the dynamo gleaming and cocked back,
The pedal treads hanging relieved
Of the boot of the law.

His cap was upside down
On the floor, next his chair.
The line of its pressure ran like a bevel
In his slightly sweating hair.

He had unstrapped
The heavy ledger, and my father
Was making tillage returns
In acres, roods, and perches.

Arithmetic and fear.
I sat staring at the polished holster
With its buttoned flap, the braid cord
Looped into the revolver butt.

'Any other root crops?
Mangolds? Marrowstems? Anything like that?'
'No.' But was there not a line
Of turnips where the seed ran out

In the potato field? I assumed
Small guilts and sat
Imagining the black hole in the barracks.
He stood up, shifted the baton-case

Further round on his belt,
Closed the domesday book,
Fitted his cap back with two hands,
And looked at me as he said goodbye.

A shadow bobbed in the window.
He was snapping the carrier spring
Over the ledger. His boot pushed off
And the bicycle ticked, ticked, ticked.

4 *Summer 1969*

While the Constabulary covered the mob
Firing into the Falls, I was suffering
Only the bullying sun of Madrid.
Each afternoon, in the casserole heat
Of the flat, as I sweated my way through
The life of Joyce, stinks from the fishmarket
Rose like the reek off a flax-dam.
At night on the balcony, gules of wine,
A sense of children in their dark corners,
Old women in black shawls near open windows,
The air a canyon rivering in Spanish.
We talked our way home over starlit plains
Where patent leather of the Guardia Civil
Gleamed like fish-bellies in flax-poisoned waters.

'Go back,' one said, 'try to touch the people.'
Another conjured Lorca from his hill.
We sat through death-counts and bullfight reports
On the television, celebrities
Arrived from where the real thing still happened.

I retreated to the cool of the Prado.
Goya's 'Shootings of the Third of May'
Covered a wall – the thrown-up arms
And spasm of the rebel, the helmeted
And knapsacked military, the efficient
Rake of the fusillade. In the next room,
His nightmares, grafted to the palace wall –
Dark cyclones, hosting, breaking; Saturn
Jewelled in the blood of his own children,

Gigantic Chaos turning his brute hips
Over the world. Also, that holmgang
Where two berserks club each other to death
For honour's sake, greaved in a bog, and sinking.

He painted with his fists and elbows, flourished
The stained cape of his heart as history charged.

6 *Exposure*

It is December in Wicklow:
Alders dripping, birches
Inheriting the last light,
The ash tree cold to look at.

A comet that was lost
Should be visible at sunset,
Those million tons of light
Like a glimmer of haws and rose-hips,

And I sometimes see a falling star.
If I could come on meteorite!
Instead I walk through damp leaves,
Husks, the spent flukes of autumn,

Imagining a hero
On some muddy compound,
His gift like a slingstone
Whirled for the desperate.

How did I end up like this?
I often think of my friends'
Beautiful prismatic counselling
And the anvil brains of some who hate me

As I sit weighing and weighing
My responsible *tristia*.
For what? For the ear? For the people?
For what is said behind-backs?

Rain comes down through the alders,
Its low conducive voices
Mutter about let-downs and erosions
And yet each drop recalls

The diamond absolutes.
I am neither internee nor informer;
An inner émigré, grown long-haired
And thoughtful; a wood-kerne

Escaped from the massacre,
Taking protective colouring
From bole and bark, feeling
Every wind that blows;

Who, blowing up these sparks
For their meagre heat, have missed
The once-in-a-lifetime portent,
The comet's pulsing rose.

Oysters

Our shells clacked on the plates.
My tongue was a filling estuary,
My palate hung with starlight:
As I tasted the salty Pleiades
Orion dipped his foot into the water.

Alive and violated,
They lay on their beds of ice:
Bivalves: the split bulb
And philandering sigh of ocean.
Millions of them ripped and shucked and scattered.

We had driven to that coast
Through flowers and limestone
And there we were, toasting friendship,
Laying down a perfect memory
In the cool of thatch and crockery.

Over the Alps, packed deep in hay and snow,
The Romans hauled their oysters south to Rome:
I saw damp panniers disgorge
The frond-lipped, brine-stung
Glut of privilege

And was angry that my trust could not repose
In the clear light, like poetry or freedom
Leaning in from sea. I ate the day
Deliberately, that its tang
Might quicken me all into verb, pure verb.

A Drink of Water

She came every morning to draw water
Like an old bat staggering up the field:
The pump's whooping cough, the bucket's clatter
And slow diminuendo as it filled,
Announced her. I recall
Her grey apron, the pocked white enamel
Of the brimming bucket, and the treble
Creak of her voice like the pump's handle.
Nights when a full moon lifted past her gable
It fell back through her window and would lie
Into the water set out on the table.
Where I have dipped to drink again, to be
Faithful to the admonishment on her cup,
Remember the Giver, fading off the lip.

The Strand at Lough Beg

in memory of Colum McCartney

> *All round this little island, on the strand*
> *Far down below there, where the breakers strive,*
> *Grow the tall rushes from the oozy sand.*
>
> DANTE, *Purgatorio*, I, 100–103

Leaving the white glow of filling stations
And a few lonely streetlamps among fields
You climbed the hills towards Newtownhamilton
Past the Fews Forest, out beneath the stars –
Along that road, a high, bare pilgrim's track
Where Sweeney fled before the bloodied heads,
Goat-beards and dogs' eyes in a demon pack
Blazing out of the ground, snapping and squealing.
What blazed ahead of you? A faked roadblock?
The red lamp swung, the sudden brakes and stalling
Engine, voices, heads hooded and the cold-nosed gun?
Or in your driving mirror, tailing headlights
That pulled out suddenly and flagged you down
Where you weren't known and far from what you knew:
The lowland clays and waters of Lough Beg,
Church Island's spire, its soft treeline of yew.

There you once heard guns fired behind the house
Long before rising time, when duck shooters
Haunted the marigolds and bulrushes,
But still were scared to find spent cartridges,
Acrid, brassy, genital, ejected,
On your way across the strand to fetch the cows.
For you and yours and yours and mine fought shy,
Spoke an old language of conspirators

And could not crack the whip or seize the day:
Big-voiced scullions, herders, feelers round
Haycocks and hindquarters, talkers in byres,
Slow arbitrators of the burial ground.

Across that strand of yours the cattle graze
Up to their bellies in an early mist
And now they turn their unbewildered gaze
To where we work our way through squeaking sedge
Drowning in dew. Like a dull blade with its edge
Honed bright, Lough Beg half-shines under the haze.
I turn because the sweeping of your feet
Has stopped behind me, to find you on your knees
With blood and roadside muck in your hair and eyes,
Then kneel in front of you in brimming grass
And gather up cold handfuls of the dew
To wash you, cousin. I dab you clean with moss
Fine as the drizzle out of a low cloud.
I lift you under the arms and lay you flat.
With rushes that shoot green again, I plait
Green scapulars to wear over your shroud.

Casualty

I

He would drink by himself
And raise a weathered thumb
Towards the high shelf,
Calling another rum
And blackcurrant, without
Having to raise his voice,
Or order a quick stout
By a lifting of the eyes
And a discreet dumb-show
Of pulling off the top;
At closing time would go
In waders and peaked cap
Into the showery dark,
A dole-kept breadwinner
But a natural for work.
I loved his whole manner,
Sure-footed but too sly,
His deadpan sidling tact,
His fisherman's quick eye
And turned, observant back.

Incomprehensible
To him, my other life.
Sometimes, on his high stool,
Too busy with his knife
At a tobacco plug
And not meeting my eye,
In the pause after a slug
He mentioned poetry.

We would be on our own
And, always politic
And shy of condescension,
I would manage by some trick
To switch the talk to eels
Or lore of the horse and cart
Or the Provisionals.

But my tentative art
His turned back watches too:
He was blown to bits
Out drinking in a curfew
Others obeyed, three nights
After they shot dead
The thirteen men in Derry.
PARAS THIRTEEN, the walls said,
BOGSIDE NIL. That Wednesday
Everybody held
Their breath and trembled.

II

It was a day of cold
Raw silence, windblown
Surplice and soutane:
Rained-on, flower-laden
Coffin after coffin
Seemed to float from the door
Of the packed cathedral
Like blossoms on slow water.
The common funeral
Unrolled its swaddling band,

Lapping, tightening
Till we were braced and bound
Like brothers in a ring.

But he would not be held
At home by his own crowd
Whatever threats were phoned,
Whatever black flags waved.
I see him as he turned
In that bombed offending place,
Remorse fused with terror
In his still knowable face,
His cornered outfaced stare
Blinding in the flash.

He had gone miles away
For he drank like a fish
Nightly, naturally
Swimming towards the lure
Of warm lit-up places,
The blurred mesh and murmur
Drifting among glasses
In the gregarious smoke.
How culpable was he
That last night when he broke
Our tribe's complicity?
'Now you're supposed to be
An educated man,'
I hear him say. 'Puzzle me
The right answer to that one.'

III

I missed his funeral,
Those quiet walkers
And sideways talkers
Shoaling out of his lane
To the respectable
Purring of the hearse . . .
They move in equal pace
With the habitual
Slow consolation
Of a dawdling engine,
The line lifted, hand
Over fist, cold sunshine
On the water, the land
Banked under fog: that morning
When he took me in his boat,
The screw purling, turning
Indolent fathoms white,
I tasted freedom with him.
To get out early, haul
Steadily off the bottom,
Dispraise the catch, and smile
As you find a rhythm
Working you, slow mile by mile,
Into your proper haunt
Somewhere, well out, beyond . . .

Dawn-sniffing revenant,
Plodder through midnight rain,
Question me again.

The Singer's House

When they said *Carrickfergus* I could hear
the frosty echo of saltminers' picks.
I imagined it, chambered and glinting,
a township built of light.

What do we say any more
to conjure the salt of our earth?
So much comes and is gone
that should be crystal and kept,

and amicable weathers
that bring up the grain of things,
their tang of season and store,
are all the packing we'll get.

So I say to myself *Gweebarra*
and its music hits off the place
like water hitting off granite.
I see the glittering sound

framed in your window,
knives and forks set on oilcloth,
and the seals' heads, suddenly outlined,
scanning everything.

People here used to believe
that drowned souls lived in the seals.
At spring tides they might change shape.
They loved music and swam in for a singer

who might stand at the end of summer
in the mouth of a whitewashed turf-shed,
his shoulder to the jamb, his song
a rowboat far out in evening.

When I came here first you were always singing,
a hint of the clip of the pick
in your winnowing climb and attack.
Raise it again, man. We still believe what we hear.

Elegy

The way we are living,
timorous or bold,
will have been our life.
Robert Lowell,

the sill geranium is lit
by the lamp I write by,
a wind from the Irish Sea
is shaking it –

here where we all sat
ten days ago, with you,
the master elegist
and welder of English.

As you swayed the talk
and rode on the swaying tiller
of yourself, ribbing me
about my fear of water,

what was not within your empery?
You drank America
like the heart's
iron vodka,

promulgating art's
deliberate, peremptory
love and arrogance.
Your eyes saw what your hand did

as you Englished Russian,
as you bullied out
heart-hammering blank sonnets
of love for Harriet

and Lizzie, and the briny
water-breaking dolphin –
your dorsal nib
gifted at last

to inveigle and to plash,
helmsman, netsman, *retiarius*.
That hand. Warding and grooming
and amphibious.

Two a.m., seaboard weather.
Not the proud sail of your great verse . . .
No. You were our night ferry
thudding in a big sea,

the whole craft ringing
with an armourer's music
the course set wilfully across
the ungovernable and dangerous.

And now a teem of rain
and the geranium tremens.
*A father's no shield
for his child* –

you found the child in me
when you took farewells
under the full bay tree
by the gate in Glanmore,

opulent and restorative
as that lingering summertime,
the fish-dart of your eyes
risking, 'I'll pray for you.'

.

from Glanmore Sonnets

for Ann Saddlemyer
'our heartiest welcomer'

II

Sensings, mountings from the hiding places,
Words entering almost the sense of touch,
Ferreting themselves out of their dark hutch –
'These things are not secrets but mysteries,'
Oisin Kelly told me years ago
In Belfast, hankering after stone
That connived with the chisel, as if the grain
Remembered what the mallet tapped to know.
Then I landed in the hedge-school of Glanmore
And from the backs of ditches hoped to raise
A voice caught back off slug-horn and slow chanter
That might continue, hold, dispel, appease:
Vowels ploughed into other, opened ground,
Each verse returning like the plough turned round.

Dogger, Rockall, Malin, Irish Sea:
Green, swift upsurges, North Atlantic flux
Conjured by that strong gale-warning voice,
Collapse into a sibilant penumbra.
Midnight and closedown. Sirens of the tundra,
Of eel-road, seal-road, keel-road, whale-road, raise
Their wind-compounded keen behind the baize
And drive the trawlers to the lee of Wicklow.
L'Etoile, *Le Guillemot*, *La Belle Hélène*
Nursed their bright names this morning in the bay
That toiled like mortar. It was marvellous
And actual, I said out loud, 'A haven,'
The word deepening, clearing, like the sky
Elsewhere on Minches, Cromarty, The Faroes.

The Otter

When you plunged
The light of Tuscany wavered
And swung through the pool
From top to bottom.

I loved your wet head and smashing crawl,
Your fine swimmer's back and shoulders
Surfacing and surfacing again
This year and every year since.

I sat dry-throated on the warm stones.
You were beyond me.
The mellowed clarities, the grape-deep air
Thinned and disappointed.

Thank God for the slow loadening,
When I hold you now
We are close and deep
As the atmosphere on water.

My two hands are plumbed water.
You are my palpable, lithe
Otter of memory
In the pool of the moment,

Turning to swim on your back,
Each silent, thigh-shaking kick
Retilting the light,
Heaving the cool at your neck.

And suddenly you're out,
Back again, intent as ever,
Heavy and frisky in your freshened pelt,
Printing the stones.

The Skunk

Up, black, striped and damasked like the chasuble
At a funeral Mass, the skunk's tail
Paraded the skunk. Night after night
I expected her like a visitor.

The refrigerator whinnied into silence.
My desk light softened beyond the verandah.
Small oranges loomed in the orange tree.
I began to be tense as a voyeur.

After eleven years I was composing
Love-letters again, broaching the word 'wife'
Like a stored cask, as if its slender vowel
Had mutated into the night earth and air

Of California. The beautiful, useless
Tang of eucalyptus spelt your absence.
The aftermath of a mouthful of wine
Was like inhaling you off a cold pillow.

And there she was, the intent and glamorous,
Ordinary, mysterious skunk,
Mythologized, demythologized,
Snuffing the boards five feet beyond me.

It all came back to me last night, stirred
By the sootfall of your things at bedtime,
Your head-down, tail-up hunt in a bottom drawer
For the black plunge-line nightdress.

Song

A rowan like a lipsticked girl.
Between the by-road and the main road
Alder trees at a wet and dripping distance
Stand off among the rushes.

There are the mud-flowers of dialect
And the immortelles of perfect pitch
And that moment when the bird sings very close
To the music of what happens.

The Harvest Bow

As you plaited the harvest bow
You implicated the mellowed silence in you
In wheat that does not rust
But brightens as it tightens twist by twist
Into a knowable corona,
A throwaway love-knot of straw.

Hands that aged round ashplants and cane sticks
And lapped the spurs on a lifetime of gamecocks
Harked to their gift and worked with fine intent
Until your fingers moved somnambulant:
I tell and finger it like braille,
Gleaning the unsaid off the palpable,

And if I spy into its golden loops
I see us walk between the railway slopes
Into an evening of long grass and midges,
Blue smoke straight up, old beds and ploughs in hedges,
An auction notice on an outhouse wall –
You with a harvest bow in your lapel,

Me with the fishing rod, already homesick
For the big lift of these evenings, as your stick
Whacking the tips off weeds and bushes
Beats out of time, and beats, but flushes
Nothing: that original townland
Still tongue-tied in the straw tied by your hand.

The end of art is peace
Could be the motto of this frail device
That I have pinned up on our deal dresser –
Like a drawn snare
Slipped lately by the spirit of the corn
Yet burnished by its passage, and still warm.

In Memoriam Francis Ledwidge

killed in France 31 July 1917

The bronze soldier hitches a bronze cape
That crumples stiffly in imagined wind
No matter how the real winds buff and sweep
His sudden hunkering run, forever craned

Over Flanders. Helmet and haversack,
The gun's firm slope from butt to bayonet,
The loyal, fallen names on the embossed plaque –
It all meant little to the worried pet

I was in nineteen forty-six or seven,
Gripping my Aunt Mary by the hand
Along the Portstewart prom, then round the crescent
To thread the Castle Walk out to the strand.

The pilot from Coleraine sailed to the coal-boat.
Courting couples rose out of the scooped dunes.
A farmer stripped to his studs and shiny waistcoat
Rolled the trousers down on his timid shins.

Francis Ledwidge, you courted at the seaside
Beyond Drogheda one Sunday afternoon.
Literary, sweet-talking, countrified,
You pedalled out the leafy road from Slane

Where you belonged, among the dolorous
And lovely: the May altar of wild flowers,
Easter water sprinkled in outhouses,
Mass-rocks and hill-top raths and raftered byres.

I think of you in your Tommy's uniform,
A haunted Catholic face, pallid and brave,
Ghosting the trenches like a bloom of hawthorn
Or silence cored from a Boyne passage-grave.

It's summer, nineteen-fifteen. I see the girl
My aunt was then, herding on the long acre.
Behind a low bush in the Dardanelles
You suck stones to make your dry mouth water.

It's nineteen-seventeen. She still herds cows
But a big strafe puts the candles out in Ypres:
'My soul is by the Boyne, cutting new meadows . . .
My country wears her confirmation dress.'

'To be called a British soldier while my country
Has no place among nations . . .' You were rent
By shrapnel six weeks later. 'I am sorry
That party politics should divide our tents.'

In you, our dead enigma, all the strains
Criss-cross in useless equilibrium
And as the wind tunes through this vigilant bronze
I hear again the sure confusing drum

You followed from Boyne water to the Balkans
But miss the twilit note your flute should sound.
You were not keyed or pitched like these true-blue ones
Though all of you consort now underground.

The Underground

There we were in the vaulted tunnel running,
You in your going-away coat speeding ahead
And me, me then like a fleet god gaining
Upon you before you turned to a reed

Or some new white flower japped with crimson
As the coat flapped wild and button after button
Sprang off and fell in a trail
Between the Underground and the Albert Hall.

Honeymooning, mooning around, late for the Proms,
Our echoes die in that corridor and now
I come as Hansel came on the moonlit stones
Retracing the path back, lifting the buttons

To end up in a draughty lamplit station
After the trains have gone, the wet track
Bared and tensed as I am, all attention
For your step following and damned if I look back.

A Hazel Stick for Catherine Ann

The living mother-of-pearl of a salmon
just out of the water

is gone just like that, but your stick
is kept salmon-silver.

Seasoned and bendy,
it convinces the hand

that what you have you hold
to play with and pose with

and lay about with.
But then too it points back to cattle

and spatter and beating
the bars of a gate –

the very stick we might cut
from your family tree.

The living cobalt of an afternoon
dragonfly drew my eye to it first

and the evening I trimmed it for you
you saw your first glow-worm –

all of us stood round in silence, even you
gigantic enough to darken the sky

for a glow-worm.
And when I poked open the grass

a tiny brightening den lit the eye
in the blunt pared end of your stick.

A Kite for Michael and Christopher

All through that Sunday afternoon
a kite flew above Sunday,
a tightened drumhead, a flitter of blown chaff.

I'd seen it grey and slippy in the making,
I'd tapped it when it dried out white and stiff,
I'd tied the bows of newspaper
along its six-foot tail.

But now it was far up like a small black lark
and now it dragged as if the bellied string
were a wet rope hauled upon
to lift a shoal.

My friend says that the human soul
is about the weight of a snipe,
yet the soul at anchor there,
the string that sags and ascends,
weighs like a furrow assumed into the heavens.

Before the kite plunges down into the wood
and this line goes useless
take in your two hands, boys, and feel
the strumming, rooted, long-tailed pull of grief.
You were born fit for it.
Stand in here in front of me
and take the strain.

The Railway Children

When we climbed the slopes of the cutting
We were eye-level with the white cups
Of the telegraph poles and the sizzling wires.

Like lovely freehand they curved for miles
East and miles west beyond us, sagging
Under their burden of swallows.

We were small and thought we knew nothing
Worth knowing. We thought words travelled the wires
In the shiny pouches of raindrops,

Each one seeded full with the light
Of the sky, the gleam of the lines, and ourselves
So infinitesimally scaled

We could stream through the eye of a needle.

from Station Island

I had come to the edge of the water,
soothed by just looking, idling over it
as if it were a clear barometer

or a mirror, when his reflection
did not appear but I sensed a presence
entering into my concentration

on not being concentrated as he spoke
my name. And though I was reluctant
I turned to meet his face and the shock

is still in me at what I saw. His brow
was blown open above the eye and blood
had dried on his neck and cheek. 'Easy now,'

he said, 'it's only me. You've seen men as raw
after a football match . . . What time it was
when I was wakened up I still don't know

but I heard this knocking, knocking, and it
scared me, like the phone in the small hours,
so I had the sense not to put on the light

but looked out from behind the curtain.
I saw two customers on the doorstep
and an old Land Rover with the doors open

parked on the street, so I let the curtain drop;
but they must have been waiting for it to move
for they shouted to come down into the shop.

She started to cry then and roll round the bed,
lamenting and lamenting to herself,
not even asking who it was. "Is your head

astray, or what's come over you?" I roared, more
to bring myself to my senses
than out of any real anger at her

for the knocking shook me, the way they kept it up,
and her whingeing and half-screeching made it worse.
All the time they were shouting, "Shop!

Shop!" so I pulled on my shoes and a sportscoat
and went back to the window and called out,
"What do you want? Could you quieten the racket

or I'll not come down at all." "There's a child not well.
Open up and see what you have got – pills
or a powder or something in a bottle,"

one of them said. He stepped back off the footpath
so I could see his face in the streetlamp
and when the other moved I knew them both.

But bad and all as the knocking was, the quiet
hit me worse. She was quiet herself now,
lying dead still, whispering to watch out.

At the bedroom door I switched on the light.
"It's odd they didn't look for a chemist.
Who are they anyway at this hour of the night?"

she asked me, with the eyes standing in her head.
"I know them to see," I said, but something
made me reach and squeeze her hand across the bed

before I went downstairs into the aisle
of the shop. I stood there, going weak
in the legs. I remember the stale smell

of cooked meat or something coming through
as I went to open up. From then on
you know as much about it as I do.'

'Did they say nothing?' 'Nothing. What would they say?'
'Were they in uniform? Not masked in any way?'
'They were barefaced as they would be in the day,

shites thinking they were the be-all and the end-all.'
'Not that it is any consolation
but they were caught,' I told him, 'and got jail.'

Big-limbed, decent, open-faced, he stood
forgetful of everything now except
whatever was welling up in his spoiled head,

beginning to smile. 'You've put on a bit of weight
since you did your courting in that big Austin
you got the loan of on a Sunday night.'

Through life and death he had hardly aged.
There always was an athlete's cleanliness
shining off him, and except for the ravaged

forehead and the blood, he was still that same
rangy midfielder in a blue jersey
and starched pants, the one stylist on the team,

the perfect, clean, unthinkable victim.
'Forgive the way I have lived indifferent –
forgive my timid circumspect involvement,'

I surprised myself by saying. 'Forgive
my eye,' he said, 'all that's above my head.'
And then a stun of pain seemed to go through him

and he trembled like a heatwave and faded.

XII

Like a convalescent, I took the hand
stretched down from the jetty, sensed again
an alien comfort as I stepped on ground

to find the helping hand still gripping mine,
fish-cold and bony, but whether to guide
or to be guided I could not be certain

for the tall man in step at my side
seemed blind, though he walked straight as a rush
upon his ashplant, his eyes fixed straight ahead.

Then I knew him in the flesh
out there on the tarmac among the cars,
wintered hard and sharp as a blackthorn bush.

His voice eddying with the vowels of all rivers
came back to me, though he did not speak yet,
a voice like a prosecutor's or a singer's,

cunning, narcotic, mimic, definite
as a steel nib's downstroke, quick and clean,
and suddenly he hit a litter basket

with his stick, saying, 'Your obligation
is not discharged by any common rite.
What you do you must do on your own.

The main thing is to write
for the joy of it. Cultivate a work-lust
that imagines its haven like your hands at night

dreaming the sun in the sunspot of a breast.
You are fasted now, light-headed, dangerous.
Take off from here. And don't be so earnest,

so ready for the sackcloth and the ashes.
Let go, let fly, forget.
You've listened long enough. Now strike your note.'

It was as if I had stepped free into space
alone with nothing that I had not known
already. Raindrops blew in my face

as I came to and heard the harangue and jeers
going on and on. 'The English language
belongs to us. You are raking at dead fires,

rehearsing the old whinges at your age.
That subject people stuff is a cod's game,
infantile, like this peasant pilgrimage.

You lose more of yourself than you redeem
doing the decent thing. Keep at a tangent.
When they make the circle wide, it's time to swim

out on your own and fill the element
with signatures on your own frequency,
echo-soundings, searches, probes, allurements,

elver-gleams in the dark of the whole sea.'
The shower broke in a cloudburst, the tarmac
fumed and sizzled. As he moved off quickly

the downpour loosed its screens round his straight walk.

Alphabets

A shadow his father makes with joined hands
And thumbs and fingers nibbles on the wall
Like a rabbit's head. He understands
He will understand more when he goes to school.

There he draws smoke with chalk the whole first week,
Then draws the forked stick that they call a Y.
This is writing. A swan's neck and swan's back
Make the 2 he can see now as well as say.

Two rafters and a cross-tie on the slate
Are the letter some call *ah*, some call *ay*.
There are charts, there are headlines, there is a right
Way to hold the pen and a wrong way.

First it is 'copying out', and then 'English',
Marked correct with a little leaning hoe.
Smells of inkwells rise in the classroom hush.
A globe in the window tilts like a coloured O.

II

Declensions sang on air like a *hosanna*
As, column after stratified column,
Book One of *Elementa Latina*,
Marbled and minatory, rose up in him.

For he was fostered next in a stricter school
Named for the patron saint of the oak wood
Where classes switched to the pealing of a bell
And he left the Latin forum for the shade

Of new calligraphy that felt like home.
The letters of this alphabet were trees.
The capitals were orchards in full bloom,
The lines of script like briars coiled in ditches.

Here in her snooded garment and bare feet,
All ringleted in assonance and woodnotes,
The poet's dream stole over him like sunlight
And passed into the tenebrous thickets.

He learns this other writing. He is the scribe
Who drove a team of quills on his white field.
Round his cell door the blackbirds dart and dab.
Then self-denial, fasting, the pure cold.

By rules that hardened the farther they reached north
He bends to his desk and begins again.
Christ's sickle has been in the undergrowth.
The script grows bare and Merovingian.

III

The globe has spun. He stands in a wooden O.
He alludes to Shakespeare. He alludes to Graves.
Time has bulldozed the school and school window.
Balers drop bales like printouts where stooked sheaves

Made lambdas on the stubble once at harvest
And the delta face of each potato pit
Was patted straight and moulded against frost.
All gone, with the omega that kept

Watch above each door, the good-luck horseshoe.
Yet shape-note language, absolute on air
As Constantine's sky-lettered IN HOC SIGNO
Can still command him; or the necromancer

Who would hang from the domed ceiling of his house
A figure of the world with colours in it
So that the figure of the universe
And 'not just single things' would meet his sight

When he walked abroad. As from his small window
The astronaut sees all he has sprung from,
The risen, aqueous, singular, lucent O
Like a magnified and buoyant ovum –

Or like my own wide pre-reflective stare
All agog at the plasterer on his ladder
Skimming our gable and writing our name there
With his trowel point, letter by strange letter.

The Haw Lantern

The wintry haw is burning out of season,
crab of the thorn, a small light for small people,
wanting no more from them but that they keep
the wick of self-respect from dying out,
not having to blind them with illumination.

But sometimes when your breath plumes in the frost
it takes the roaming shape of Diogenes
with his lantern, seeking one just man;
so you end up scrutinized from behind the haw
he holds up at eye-level on its twig,
and you flinch before its bonded pith and stone,
its blood-prick that you wish would test and clear you,
its pecked-at ripeness that scans you, then moves on.

From the Republic of Conscience

I

When I landed in the republic of conscience
it was so noiseless when the engines stopped
I could hear a curlew high above the runway.

At immigration, the clerk was an old man
who produced a wallet from his homespun coat
and showed me a photograph of my grandfather.

The woman in customs asked me to declare
the words of our traditional cures and charms
to heal dumbness and avert the evil eye.

No porters. No interpreter. No taxi.
You carried your own burden and very soon
your symptoms of creeping privilege disappeared.

II

Fog is a dreaded omen there but lightning
spells universal good and parents hang
swaddled infants in trees during thunderstorms.

Salt is their precious mineral. And seashells
are held to the ear during births and funerals.
The base of all inks and pigments is seawater.

Their sacred symbol is a stylized boat.
The sail is an ear, the mast a sloping pen,
the hull a mouth-shape, the keel an open eye.

At their inauguration, public leaders
must swear to uphold unwritten law and weep
to atone for their presumption to hold office –

and to affirm their faith that all life sprang
from salt in tears which the sky-god wept
after he dreamt his solitude was endless.

III

I came back from that frugal republic
with my two arms the one length, the customs woman
having insisted my allowance was myself.

The old man rose and gazed into my face
and said that was official recognition
that I was now a dual citizen.

He therefore desired me when I got home
to consider myself a representative
and to speak on their behalf in my own tongue.

Their embassies, he said, were everywhere
but operated independently
and no ambassador would ever be relieved.

The Stone Verdict

When he stands in the judgement place
With his stick in his hand and the broad hat
Still on his head, maimed by self-doubt
And an old disdain of sweet talk and excuses,
It will be no justice if the sentence is blabbed out.
He will expect more than words in the ultimate court
He relied on through a lifetime's speechlessness.

Let it be like the judgement of Hermes,
God of the stone heap, where the stones were verdicts
Cast solidly at his feet, piling up around him
Until he stood waist-deep in the cairn
Of his absolution: maybe a gate-pillar
Or a tumbled wallstead where hogweed earths the silence
Somebody will break at last to say, 'Here
His spirit lingers,' and will have said too much.

from Clearances

in memoriam M.K.H., 1911–1984

3

When all the others were away at Mass
I was all hers as we peeled potatoes.
They broke the silence, let fall one by one
Like solder weeping off the soldering iron:
Cold comforts set between us, things to share
Gleaming in a bucket of clean water.
And again let fall. Little pleasant splashes
From each other's work would bring us to our senses.

So while the parish priest at her bedside
Went hammer and tongs at the prayers for the dying
And some were responding and some crying
I remembered her head bent towards my head,
Her breath in mine, our fluent dipping knives –
Never closer the whole rest of our lives.

In the last minutes he said more to her
Almost than in all their life together.
'You'll be in New Row on Monday night
And I'll come up for you and you'll be glad
When I walk in the door . . . Isn't that right?'
His head was bent down to her propped-up head.
She could not hear but we were overjoyed.
He called her good and girl. Then she was dead,
The searching for a pulsebeat was abandoned
And we all knew one thing by being there.
The space we stood around had been emptied
Into us to keep, it penetrated
Clearances that suddenly stood open.
High cries were felled and a pure change happened.

The Wishing Tree

I thought of her as the wishing tree that died
And saw it lifted, root and branch, to heaven,
Trailing a shower of all that had been driven

Need by need by need into its hale
Sap-wood and bark: coin and pin and nail
Came streaming from it like a comet-tail

New-minted and dissolved. I had a vision
Of an airy branch-head rising through damp cloud,
Of turned-up faces where the tree had stood.

from The Cure at Troy

Human beings suffer.
They torture one another.
They get hurt and get hard.
No poem or play or song
Can fully right a wrong
Inflicted and endured.

History says, Don't hope
On this side of the grave,
But then, once in a lifetime
The longed-for tidal wave
Of justice can rise up,
And hope and history rhyme.

So hope for a great sea-change
On the far side of revenge.
Believe that a farther shore
Is reachable from here.
Believe in miracles
And cures and healing wells.

Call miracle self-healing,
The utter self-revealing
Double-take of feeling.
If there's fire on the mountain
And lightning and storm
And a god speaks from the sky

That means someone is hearing
The outcry and the birth-cry
Of new life at its term.
It means once in a lifetime
That justice can rise up
And hope and history rhyme.

Markings

I

We marked the pitch: four jackets for four goalposts,
That was all. The corners and the squares
Were there like longitude and latitude
Under the bumpy ground, to be
Agreed about or disagreed about
When the time came. And then we picked the teams
And crossed the line our called names drew between us.

Youngsters shouting their heads off in a field
As the light died and they kept on playing
Because by then they were playing in their heads
And the actual kicked ball came to them
Like a dream heaviness, and their own hard
Breathing in the dark and skids on grass
Sounded like effort in another world . . .
It was quick and constant, a game that never need
Be played out. Some limit had been passed,
There was fleetness, furtherance, untiredness
In time that was extra, unforeseen and free.

II

You also loved lines pegged out in the garden,
The spade nicking the first straight edge along
The tight white string. Or string stretched perfectly
To make the outline of a house foundation,
Pale timber battens set at right angles
For every corner, each freshly sawn new board
Spick and span in the oddly passive grass.

Or the imaginary line straight down
A field of grazing, to be ploughed open
From the rod stuck in one headrig to the rod
Stuck in the other.

III

All these things entered you
As if they were both the door and what came through it.
They marked the spot, marked time and held it open.
A mower parted the bronze sea of corn.
A windlass hauled the centre out of water.
Two men with a cross-cut kept it swimming
Into a felled beech backwards and forwards
So that they seemed to row the steady earth.

Seeing Things

Inishbofin on a Sunday morning.
Sunlight, turfsmoke, seagulls, boatslip, diesel.
One by one we were being handed down
Into a boat that dipped and shilly-shallied
Scaresomely every time. We sat tight
On short cross-benches, in nervous twos and threes,
Obedient, newly close, nobody speaking
Except the boatmen, as the gunwales sank
And seemed they might ship water any minute.
The sea was very calm but even so,
When the engine kicked and our ferryman
Swayed for balance, reaching for the tiller,
I panicked at the shiftiness and heft
Of the craft itself. What guaranteed us –
That quick response and buoyancy and swim –
Kept me in agony. All the time
As we went sailing evenly across
The deep, still, seeable-down-into water,
It was as if I looked from another boat
Sailing through air, far up, and could see
How riskily we fared into the morning,
And loved in vain our bare, bowed, numbered heads.

II

Claritas. The dry-eyed Latin word
Is perfect for the carved stone of the water
Where Jesus stands up to his unwet knees
And John the Baptist pours out more water
Over his head: all this in bright sunlight
On the façade of a cathedral. Lines
Hard and thin and sinuous represent
The flowing river. Down between the lines
Little antic fish are all go. Nothing else.
And yet in that utter visibility
The stone's alive with what's invisible:
Waterweed, stirred sand-grains hurrying off,
The shadowy, unshadowed stream itself.
All afternoon, heat wavered on the steps
And the air we stood up to our eyes in wavered
Like the zig-zag hieroglyph for life itself.

III

Once upon a time my undrowned father
Walked into our yard. He had gone to spray
Potatoes in a field on the riverbank
And wouldn't bring me with him. The horse-sprayer
Was too big and new-fangled, bluestone might
Burn me in the eyes, the horse was fresh, I
Might scare the horse, and so on. I threw stones
At a bird on the shed roof, as much for
The clatter of the stones as anything,
But when he came back, I was inside the house
And saw him out the window, scatter-eyed
And daunted, strange without his hat,
His step unguided, his ghosthood immanent.
When he was turning on the riverbank,
The horse had rusted and reared up and pitched
Cart and sprayer and everything off balance
So the whole rig went over into a deep
Whirlpool, hoofs, chains, shafts, cartwheels, barrel
And tackle, all tumbling off the world,
And the hat already merrily swept along
The quieter reaches. That afternoon
I saw him face to face, he came to me
With his damp footprints out of the river,
And there was nothing between us there
That might not still be happily ever after.

1. I. 87

Dangerous pavements.
But I face the ice this year
With my father's stick.

Field of Vision

I remember this woman who sat for years
In a wheelchair, looking straight ahead
Out the window at sycamore trees unleafing
And leafing at the far end of the lane.

Straight out past the TV in the corner,
The stunted, agitated hawthorn bush,
The same small calves with their backs to wind and rain,
The same acre of ragwort, the same mountain.

She was steadfast as the big window itself.
Her brow was clear as the chrome bits of the chair.
She never lamented once and she never
Carried a spare ounce of emotional weight.

Face to face with her was an education
Of the sort you got across a well-braced gate –
One of those lean, clean, iron, roadside ones
Between two whitewashed pillars, where you could see

Deeper into the country than you expected
And discovered that the field behind the hedge
Grew more distinctly strange as you kept standing
Focused and drawn in by what barred the way.

from Glanmore Revisited

VII *The Skylight*

You were the one for skylights. I opposed
Cutting into the seasoned tongue-and-groove
Of pitch pine. I liked it low and closed,
Its claustrophobic, nest-up-in-the-roof
Effect. I liked the snuff-dry feeling,
The perfect, trunk-lid fit of the old ceiling.
Under there, it was all hutch and hatch.
The blue slates kept the heat like midnight thatch.

But when the slates came off, extravagant
Sky entered and held surprise wide open.
For days I felt like an inhabitant
Of that house where the man sick of the palsy
Was lowered through the roof, had his sins forgiven,
Was healed, took up his bed and walked away.

A Pillowed Head

Matutinal. Mother-of-pearl
Summer come early. Slashed carmines
And washed milky blues.

To be first on the road,
Up with the ground-mists and pheasants.
To be older and grateful

That this time you too were half-grateful
The pangs had begun – prepared
And clear-headed, foreknowing

The trauma, entering on it
With full consent of the will.
(The first time, dismayed and arrayed

In your cut-off white cotton gown,
You were more bride than earth-mother
Up on the stirrup-rigged bed,

Who were self-possessed now
To the point of a walk on the pier
Before you checked in.)

And then later on I half-fainted
When the little slapped palpable girl
Was handed to me; but as usual

Came to in two wide-open eyes
That had been dawned into farther
Than ever, and had outseen the last

Of all of those mornings of waiting
When your domed brow was one long held silence
And the dawn chorus anything but.

Fosterling

'That heavy greenness fostered by water'
JOHN MONTAGUE

At school I loved one picture's heavy greenness –
Horizons rigged with windmills' arms and sails.
The millhouses' still outlines. Their in-placeness
Still more in place when mirrored in canals.
I can't remember not ever having known
The immanent hydraulics of a land
Of *glar* and *glit* and floods at *dailigone*.
My silting hope. My lowlands of the mind.

Heaviness of being. And poetry
Sluggish in the doldrums of what happens.
Me waiting until I was nearly fifty
To credit marvels. Like the tree-clock of tin cans
The tinkers made. So long for air to brighten,
Time to be dazzled and the heart to lighten.

from Lightenings

The annals say: when the monks of Clonmacnoise
Were all at prayers inside the oratory
A ship appeared above them in the air.

The anchor dragged along behind so deep
It hooked itself into the altar rails
And then, as the big hull rocked to a standstill,

A crewman shinned and grappled down the rope
And struggled to release it. But in vain.
'This man can't bear our life here and will drown,'

The abbot said, 'unless we help him.' So
They did, the freed ship sailed, and the man climbed back
Out of the marvellous as he had known it.

from Crossings

Everything flows. Even a solid man,
A pillar to himself and to his trade,
All yellow boots and stick and soft felt hat,

Can sprout wings at the ankle and grow fleet
As the god of fair days, stone posts, roads and crossroads,
Guardian of travellers and psychopomp.

'Look for a man with an ashplant on the boat,'
My father told his sister setting out
For London, 'and stay near him all night

And you'll be safe.' Flow on, flow on
The journey of the soul with its soul guide
And the mysteries of dealing-men with sticks!

The Rain Stick

for Beth and Rand

Up-end the rain stick and what happens next
Is a music that you never would have known
To listen for. In a cactus stalk

Downpour, sluice-rush, spillage and backwash
Come flowing through. You stand there like a pipe
Being played by water, you shake it again lightly

And diminuendo runs through all its scales
Like a gutter stopping trickling. And now here comes
A sprinkle of drops out of the freshened leaves,

Then subtle little wets off grass and daisies;
Then glitter-drizzle, almost-breaths of air.
Up-end the stick again. What happens next

Is undiminished for having happened once,
Twice, ten, a thousand times before.
Who cares if all the music that transpires

Is the fall of grit or dry seeds through a cactus?
You are like a rich man entering heaven
Through the ear of a raindrop. Listen now again.

A Sofa in the Forties

All of us on the sofa in a line, kneeling
Behind each other, eldest down to youngest,
Elbows going like pistons, for this was a train

And between the jamb-wall and the bedroom door
Our speed and distance were inestimable.
First we shunted, then we whistled, then

Somebody collected the invisible
For tickets and very gravely punched it
As carriage after carriage under us

Moved faster, *chooka-chook*, the sofa legs
Went giddy and the unreachable ones
Far out on the kitchen floor began to wave.

*

Ghost-train? Death-gondola? The carved, curved ends,
Black leatherette and ornate gauntness of it
Made it seem the sofa had achieved

Flotation. Its castors on tiptoe,
Its braid and fluent backboard gave it airs
Of superannuated pageantry:

When visitors endured it, straight-backed,
When it stood off in its own remoteness,
When the insufficient toys appeared on it

On Christmas mornings, it held out as itself,
Potentially heavenbound, earthbound for sure,
Among things that might add up or let you down.

*

We entered history and ignorance
Under the wireless shelf. *Yippee-i-ay,*
Sang 'The Riders of the Range'. HERE IS THE NEWS,

Said the absolute speaker. Between him and us
A great gulf was fixed where pronunciation
Reigned tyrannically. The aerial wire

Swept from a treetop down in through a hole
Bored in the windowframe. When it moved in wind,
The sway of language and its furtherings

Swept and swayed in us like nets in water
Or the abstract, lonely curve of distant trains
As we entered history and ignorance.

*

We occupied our seats with all our might,
Fit for the uncomfortableness.
Constancy was its own reward already.

Out in front, on the big upholstered arm,
Somebody craned to the side, driver or
Fireman, wiping his dry brow with the air

Of one who had run the gauntlet. We were
The last thing on his mind, it seemed; we sensed
A tunnel coming up where we'd pour through

Like unlit carriages through fields at night,
Our only job to sit, eyes straight ahead,
And be transported and make engine noise.

Keeping Going

for Hugh

The piper coming from far away is you
With a whitewash brush for a sporran
Wobbling round you, a kitchen chair
Upside down on your shoulder, your right arm
Pretending to tuck the bag beneath your elbow,
Your pop-eyes and big cheeks nearly bursting
With laughter, but keeping the drone going on
Interminably, between catches of breath.

*

The whitewash brush. An old blanched skirted thing
On the back of the byre door, biding its time
Until spring airs spelled lime in a work-bucket
And a potstick to mix it in with water.
Those smells brought tears to the eyes, we inhaled
A kind of greeny burning and thought of brimstone.
But the slop of the actual job
Of brushing walls, the watery grey
Being lashed on in broad swatches, then drying out
Whiter and whiter, all that worked like magic.
Where had we come from, what was this kingdom
We knew we'd been restored to? Our shadows
Moved on the wall and a tar border glittered
The full length of the house, a black divide
Like a freshly opened, pungent, reeking trench.

*

Piss at the gable, the dead will congregate.
But separately. The women after dark,
Hunkering there a moment before bedtime,
The only time the soul was let alone,
The only time that face and body calmed
In the eye of heaven.
                              Buttermilk and urine,
The pantry, the housed beasts, the listening bedroom.
We were all together there in a foretime,
In a knowledge that might not translate beyond
Those wind-heaved midnights we still cannot be sure
Happened or not. It smelled of hill-fort clay
And cattle dung. When the thorn tree was cut down
You broke your arm. I shared the dread
When a strange bird perched for days on the byre roof.

*

That scene, with Macbeth helpless and desperate
In his nightmare – when he meets the hags again
And sees the apparitions in the pot –
I felt at home with that one all right. Hearth,
Steam and ululation, the smoky hair
Curtaining a cheek. 'Don't go near bad boys
In that college that you're bound for. Do you hear me?
Do you hear me speaking to you? Don't forget!'
And then the potstick quickening the gruel,
The steam crown swirled, everything intimate
And fear-swathed brightening for a moment,
Then going dull and fatal and away.

*

Grey matter like gruel flecked with blood
In spatters on the whitewash. A clean spot
Where his head had been, other stains subsumed
In the parched wall he leant his back against
That morning like any other morning,
Part-time reservist, toting his lunch-box.
A car came slow down Castle Street, made the halt,
Crossed the Diamond, slowed again and stopped
Level with him, although it was not his lift.
And then he saw an ordinary face
For what it was and a gun in his own face.
His right leg was hooked back, his sole and heel
Against the wall, his right knee propped up steady,
So he never moved, just pushed with all his might
Against himself, then fell past the tarred strip,
Feeding the gutter with his copious blood.

*

My dear brother, you have good stamina.
You stay on where it happens. Your big tractor
Pulls up at the Diamond, you wave at people,
You shout and laugh above the revs, you keep
Old roads open by driving on the new ones.
You called the piper's sporrans whitewash brushes
And then dressed up and marched us through the kitchen,
But you cannot make the dead walk or right wrong.
I see you at the end of your tether sometimes,
In the milking parlour, holding yourself up
Between two cows until your turn goes past,
Then coming to in the smell of dung again
And wondering, is this all? As it was
In the beginning, is now and shall be?
Then rubbing your eyes and seeing our old brush
Up on the byre door, and keeping going.

Two Lorries

It's raining on black coal and warm wet ashes.
There are tyre-marks in the yard, Agnew's old lorry
Has all its cribs down and Agnew the coalman
With his Belfast accent's sweet-talking my mother.
Would she ever go to a film in Magherafelt?
But it's raining and he still has half the load

To deliver farther on. This time the lode
Our coal came from was silk-black, so the ashes
Will be the silkiest white. The Magherafelt
(Via Toomebridge) bus goes by. The half-stripped lorry
With its emptied, folded coal-bags moves my mother:
The tasty ways of a leather-aproned coalman!

And films no less! The conceit of a coalman . . .
She goes back in and gets out the black lead
And emery paper, this nineteen-forties mother,
All business round her stove, half-wiping ashes
With a backhand from her cheek as the bolted lorry
Gets revved and turned and heads for Magherafelt

And the last delivery. Oh, Magherafelt!
Oh, dream of red plush and a city coalman
As time fastforwards and a different lorry
Groans into shot, up Broad Street, with a payload
That will blow the bus station to dust and ashes . . .
After that happened, I'd a vision of my mother,

A revenant on the bench where I would meet her
In that cold-floored waiting-room in Magherafelt,
Her shopping bags full up with shovelled ashes.
Death walked out past her like a dust-faced coalman
Refolding body-bags, plying his load
Empty upon empty, in a flurry

Of motes and engine-revs, but which lorry
Was it now? Young Agnew's or that other,
Heavier, deadlier one, set to explode
In a time beyond her time in Magherafelt . . .
So tally bags and sweet-talk darkness, coalman.
Listen to the rain spit in new ashes

As you heft a load of dust that was Magherafelt,
Then reappear from your lorry as my mother's
Dreamboat coalman filmed in silk-white ashes.

St Kevin and the Blackbird

And then there was St Kevin and the blackbird.
The saint is kneeling, arms stretched out, inside
His cell, but the cell is narrow, so

One turned-up palm is out the window, stiff
As a crossbeam, when a blackbird lands
And lays in it and settles down to nest.

Kevin feels the warm eggs, the small breast, the tucked
Neat head and claws and, finding himself linked
Into the network of eternal life,

Is moved to pity: now he must hold his hand
Like a branch out in the sun and rain for weeks
Until the young are hatched and fledged and flown.

*

And since the whole thing's imagined anyhow,
Imagine being Kevin. Which is he?
Self-forgetful or in agony all the time

From the neck on out down through his hurting forearms?
Are his fingers sleeping? Does he still feel his knees?
Or has the shut-eyed blank of underearth

Crept up through him? Is there distance in his head?
Alone and mirrored clear in love's deep river,
'To labour and not to seek reward,' he prays,

A prayer his body makes entirely
For he has forgotten self, forgotten bird
And on the riverbank forgotten the river's name.

The Gravel Walks

River gravel. In the beginning, that.
High summer, and the angler's motorbike
Deep in roadside flowers, like a fallen knight
Whose ghost we'd lately questioned: 'Any luck?'

As the engines of the world prepared, green nuts
Dangled and clustered closer to the whirlpool.
The trees dipped down. The flints and sandstone-bits
Worked themselves smooth and smaller in a sparkle

Of shallow, hurrying barley-sugar water
Where minnows schooled that we scared when we played –
An eternity that ended once a tractor
Dropped its link-box in the gravel bed

And cement mixers began to come to life
And men in dungarees, like captive shades,
Mixed concrete, loaded, wheeled, turned, wheeled, as if
The Pharaoh's brickyards burned inside their heads.

*

Hoard and praise the verity of gravel.
Gems for the undeluded. Milt of earth.
Its plain, champing song against the shovel
Soundtests and sandblasts words like 'honest worth'.

Beautiful in or out of the river,
The kingdom of gravel was inside you too –
Deep down, far back, clear water running over
Pebbles of caramel, hailstone, mackerel-blue.

But the actual washed stuff kept you slow and steady
As you went stooping with your barrow full
Into an absolution of the body,
The shriven life tired bones and marrow feel.

So walk on air against your better judgement
Establishing yourself somewhere in between
Those solid batches mixed with grey cement
And a tune called 'The Gravel Walks' that conjures green.

A Call

'Hold on,' she said, 'I'll just run out and get him.
The weather here's so good, he took the chance
To do a bit of weeding.'
                              So I saw him
Down on his hands and knees beside the leek rig,
Touching, inspecting, separating one
Stalk from the other, gently pulling up
Everything not tapered, frail and leafless,
Pleased to feel each little weed-root break,
But rueful also . . .
                              Then found myself listening to
The amplified grave ticking of hall clocks
Where the phone lay unattended in a calm
Of mirror glass and sunstruck pendulums . . .

And found myself then thinking: if it were nowadays,
This is how Death would summon Everyman.

Next thing he spoke and I nearly said I loved him.

A Dog Was Crying Tonight in Wicklow Also

in memory of Donatus Nwoga

When human beings found out about death
They sent the dog to Chukwu with a message:
They wanted to be let back to the house of life.
They didn't want to end up lost forever
Like burnt wood disappearing into smoke
Or ashes that get blown away to nothing.
Instead, they saw their souls in a flock at twilight
Cawing and headed back for the same old roosts
And the same bright airs and wing-stretchings
    each morning.
Death would be like a night spent in the wood:
At first light they'd be back in the house of life.
(The dog was meant to tell all this to Chukwu.)

But death and human beings took second place
When he trotted off the path and started barking
At another dog in broad daylight just barking
Back at him from the far bank of a river.

And that is how the toad reached Chukwu first,
The toad who'd overheard in the beginning
What the dog was meant to tell. 'Human beings,'
    he said
(And here the toad was trusted absolutely),
'Human beings want death to last forever.'

Then Chukwu saw the people's souls in birds
Coming towards him like black spots off the sunset
To a place where there would be neither roosts nor trees
Nor any way back to the house of life.
And his mind reddened and darkened all at once
And nothing that the dog would tell him later
Could change that vision. Great chiefs and great loves
In obliterated light, the toad in mud,
The dog crying out all night behind the corpse house.

At the Wellhead

Your songs, when you sing them with your two eyes closed
As you always do, are like a local road
We've known every turn of in the past –
That midge-veiled, high-hedged side-road where you stood
Looking and listening until a car
Would come and go and leave you lonelier
Than you had been to begin with. So, sing on,
Dear shut-eyed one, dear far-voiced veteran,

Sing yourself to where the singing comes from,
Ardent and cut off like our blind neighbour
Who played the piano all day in her bedroom.
Her notes came out to us like hoisted water
Ravelling off a bucket at the wellhead
Where next thing we'd be listening, hushed and awkward.

*

That blind-from-birth, sweet-voiced, withdrawn musician
Was like a silver vein in heavy clay.
Night water glittering in the light of day.
But also just our neighbour, Rosie Keenan.
She touched our cheeks. She let us touch her braille
In books like books wallpaper patterns came in.
Her hands were active and her eyes were full
Of open darkness and a watery shine.

She knew us by our voices. She'd say she 'saw'
Whoever or whatever. Being with her
Was intimate and helpful, like a cure

You didn't notice happening. When I read
A poem with Keenan's well in it, she said,
'I can see the sky at the bottom of it now.'

At Banagher

Then all of a sudden there appears to me
The journeyman tailor who was my antecedent:
Up on a table, cross-legged, ripping out

A garment he must recut or resew,
His lips tight back, a thread between his teeth,
Keeping his counsel always, giving none,

His eyelids steady as wrinkled horn or iron.
Self-absenting, both migrant and ensconced;
Admitted into kitchens, into clothes

His touch has the power to turn to cloth again –
All of a sudden he appears to me,
Unopen, unmendacious, unillumined.

*

So more power to him on the job there, ill at ease
Under my scrutiny in spite of years
Of being inscrutable as he threaded needles

Or matched the facings, linings, hems and seams.
He holds the needle just off centre, squinting,
And licks the thread and licks and sweeps it through,

Then takes his time to draw both ends out even,
Plucking them sharply twice. Then back to stitching.
Does he ever question what it all amounts to

Or ever will? Or care where he lays his head?
My Lord Buddha of Banagher, the way
Is opener for your being in it.

Postscript

And some time make the time to drive out west
Into County Clare, along the Flaggy Shore,
In September or October, when the wind
And the light are working off each other
So that the ocean on one side is wild
With foam and glitter, and inland among stones
The surface of a slate-grey lake is lit
By the earthed lightning of a flock of swans,
Their feathers roughed and ruffling, white on white,
Their fully grown headstrong-looking heads
Tucked or cresting or busy underwater.
Useless to think you'll park and capture it
More thoroughly. You are neither here nor there,
A hurry through which known and strange things pass
As big soft buffetings come at the car sideways
And catch the heart off guard and blow it open.

from Out of the Bag

All of us came in Doctor Kerlin's bag.
He'd arrive with it, disappear to the room
And by the time he'd reappear to wash

Those nosy, rosy, big, soft hands of his
In the scullery basin, its lined insides
(The colour of a spaniel's inside lug)

Were empty for all to see, the trap-sprung mouth
Unsnibbed and gaping wide. Then like a hypnotist
Unwinding us, he'd wind the instruments

Back into their lining, tie the cloth
Like an apron round itself,
Darken the door and leave

With the bag in his hand, a plump ark by the keel . . .
Until the next time came and in he'd come
In his fur-lined collar that was also spaniel-coloured

And go stooping up to the room again, a whiff
Of disinfectant, a Dutch interior gleam
Of waistcoat satin and highlights on the forceps.

Getting the water ready, that was next –
Not plumping hot, and not lukewarm, but soft,
Sud-luscious, saved for him from the rain-butt

And savoured by him afterwards, all thanks
Denied as he towelled hard and fast,
Then held his arms out suddenly behind him

To be squired and silk-lined into the camel coat.
At which point he once turned his eyes upon me,
Hyperborean, beyond-the-north-wind blue,

Two peepholes to the locked room I saw into
Every time his name was mentioned, skimmed
Milk and ice, swabbed porcelain, the white

And chill of tiles, steel hooks, chrome surgery tools
And blood dreeps in the sawdust where it thickened
At the foot of each cold wall. And overhead

The little, pendent, teat-hued infant parts
Strung neatly from a line up near the ceiling –
A toe, a foot and shin, an arm, a cock

A bit like the rosebud in his buttonhole.

4

The room I came from and the rest of us all came from
Stays pure reality where I stand alone,
Standing the passage of time, and she's asleep

In sheets put on for the doctor, wedding presents
That showed up again and again, bridal
And usual and useful at births and deaths.

Me at the bedside, incubating for real,
Peering, appearing to her as she closes
And opens her eyes, then lapses back

Into a faraway smile whose precinct of vision
I would enter every time, to assist and be asked
In that hoarsened whisper of triumph,

'And what do you think
Of the new wee baby the doctor brought for us all
When I was asleep?'

The Clothes Shrine

It was a whole new sweetness
In the early days to find
Light white muslin blouses
On a see-through nylon line
Drip-drying in the bathroom
Or a nylon slip in the shine
Of its own electricity –
As if St Brigid once more
Had rigged up a ray of sun
Like the one she'd strung on air
To dry her own cloak on
(Hard-pressed Brigid, so
Unstoppably on the go) –
The damp and slump and unfair
Drag of the workaday
Made light of and got through
As usual, brilliantly.

from Sonnets from Hellas

1 *Into Arcadia*

It was opulence and amen on the mountain road.
Walnuts bought on a high pass from a farmer
Who'd worked in Melbourne once and now trained water
Through a system of pipes and runnels of split reed
Known in Hellas, probably, since Hesiod –
That was the least of it. When we crossed the border
From Argos into Arcadia, and farther
Into Arcadia, a lorry-load
Of apples had burst open on the road
So that for yards our tyres raunched and scrunched them
But we drove on, juiced up and fleshed and spattered,
Revelling in it. And then it was the goatherd
With his goats in the forecourt of the filling station,
Subsisting beyond eclogue and translation.

Anahorish 1944

'We were killing pigs when the Americans arrived.
A Tuesday morning, sunlight and gutter-blood
Outside the slaughterhouse. From the main road
They would have heard the squealing,
Then heard it stop and had a view of us
In our gloves and aprons coming down the hill.
Two lines of them, guns on their shoulders, marching.
Armoured cars and tanks and open jeeps.
Sunburnt hands and arms. Unknown, unnamed,
Hosting for Normandy.
                    Not that we knew then
Where they were headed, standing there like youngsters
As they tossed us gum and tubes of coloured sweets.'

Anything Can Happen

after Horace, Odes, *I, 34*

Anything can happen. You know how Jupiter
Will mostly wait for clouds to gather head
Before he hurls the lightning? Well, just now
He galloped his thunder cart and his horses

Across a clear blue sky. It shook the earth
And the clogged underearth, the River Styx,
The winding streams, the Atlantic shore itself.
Anything can happen, the tallest towers

Be overturned, those in high places daunted,
Those overlooked regarded. Stropped-beak Fortune
Swoops, making the air gasp, tearing the crest off one,
Setting it down bleeding on the next.

Ground gives. The heaven's weight
Lifts up off Atlas like a kettle-lid.
Capstones shift, nothing resettles right.
Telluric ash and fire-spores boil away.

Helmet

Bobby Breen's. His Boston fireman's gift
With BREEN in scarlet letters on its spread
Fantailing brim,

Tinctures of sweat and hair oil
In the withered sponge and shock-absorbing webs
Beneath the crown –

Or better say the crest, for crest it is –
Leather-trimmed, steel-ridged, hand-tooled, hand-sewn,
Tipped with a little bud of beaten copper . . .

Bobby Breen's badged helmet's on my shelf
These twenty years, 'the headgear
Of the tribe', as O'Grady called it

In right heroic mood that afternoon
When the fireman-poet presented it to me
As 'the visiting fireman' –

As if I were up to it, as if I had
Served time under it, his fire-thane's shield,
His shoulder-awning, while shattering glass

And rubble-bolts out of a burning roof
Hailed down on every hatchet man and hose man there
Till the hard-reared shield-wall broke.

District and Circle

Tunes from a tin whistle underground
Curled up a corridor I'd be walking down
To where I knew I was always going to find
My watcher on the tiles, cap by his side,
His fingers perked, his two eyes eyeing me
In an unaccusing look I'd not avoid,
Or not just yet, since both were out to see
For ourselves.
              As the music larked and capered
I'd trigger and untrigger a hot coin
Held at the ready, but now my gaze was lowered
For was our traffic not in recognition?
Accorded passage, I would re-pocket and nod,
And he, still eyeing me, would also nod.

*

Posted, eyes front, along the dreamy ramparts
Of escalators ascending and descending
To a monotonous slight rocking in the works,
We were moved along, upstanding.
Elsewhere, underneath, an engine powered,
Rumbled, quickened, evened, quieted.
The white tiles gleamed. In passages that flowed
With draughts from cooler tunnels, I missed the light
Of all-overing, long since mysterious day,
Parks at lunchtime where the sunners lay
On body-heated mown grass regardless,
A resurrection scene minutes before
The resurrection, habitués
Of their garden of delights, of staggered summer.

[144]

Another level down, the platform thronged.
I re-entered the safety of numbers,
A crowd half straggle-ravelled and half strung
Like a human chain, the pushy newcomers
Jostling and purling underneath the vault,
On their marks to be first through the doors,
Street-loud, then succumbing to herd-quiet . . .
Had I betrayed or not, myself or him?
Always new to me, always familiar,
This unrepentant, now repentant turn
As I stood waiting, glad of a first tremor,
Then caught up in the now-or-never whelm
Of one and all the full length of the train.

Stepping on to it across the gap,
On to the carriage metal, I reached to grab
The stubby black roof-wort and take my stand
From planted ball of heel to heel of hand
As sweet traction and heavy down-slump stayed me.
I was on my way, well girded, yet on edge,
Spot-rooted, buoyed, aloof,
Listening to the dwindling noises off,
My back to the unclosed door, the platform empty;
And wished it could have lasted,
That long between-times pause before the budge
And glaze-over, when any forwardness
Was unwelcome and bodies readjusted,
Blindsided to themselves and other bodies.

So deeper into it, crowd-swept, strap-hanging,
My lofted arm a-swivel like a flail,
My father's glazed face in my own waning
And craning . . .
                                Again the growl
Of shutting doors, the jolt and one-off treble
Of iron on iron, then a long centrifugal
Haulage of speed through every dragging socket.

And so by night and day to be transported
Through galleried earth with them, the only relict
Of all that I belonged to, hurtled forward,
Reflecting in a window mirror-backed
By blasted weeping rock-walls.
                                Flicker-lit.

Midnight Anvil

If I wasn't there
When Barney Devlin hammered
The midnight anvil
I can still hear it: twelve blows
Struck for the millennium.

*

His nephew heard it
In Edmonton, Alberta:
The cellular phone
Held high as a horse's ear,
Barney smiling to himself.

*

Afterwards I thought
Church bels beyond the starres heard
And then imagined
Barney putting it to me:
'You'll maybe write a poem.'

*

What I'll do instead
Is quote those waterburning
Medieval smiths:
'Huf, puf! Lus, bus! Col!' *Such noise
On nights heard no one never.*

*

And Eoghan Rua
Asking Séamus MacGearailt
To forge him a spade
Sharp, well shaped from the anvil,
And ringing sweet as a bell.

The Lift

A first green braird: the hawthorn half in leaf.
Her funeral filled the road
And could have stepped from some old photograph

Of a Breton *pardon*, remote
Familiar women and men in caps
Walking four abreast, soon falling quiet.

Then came the throttle and articulated whops
Of a helicopter crossing, and afterwards
Awareness of the sound of our own footsteps,

Of open air, and the life behind those words
'Open' and 'air'. I remembered her aghast,
Foetal, shaking, sweating, shrunk, wet-haired,

A beaten breath, a misting mask, the flash
Of one wild glance, like ghost surveillance
From behind a gleam of helicopter glass.

A lifetime, then the deathtime: reticence
Keeping us together when together,
All declaration deemed outspokenness.

Favourite aunt, good sister, faithful daughter,
Delicate since childhood, tough alloy
Of disapproval, kindness and *hauteur*,

She took the risk, at last, of certain joys –
Her birdtable and jubilating birds,
The 'fashion' in her wardrobe and her tallboy.

Weather, in the end, would say our say.
Reprise of griefs in summer's clearest mornings,
Children's deaths in snowdrops and the may,

Whole requiems at the sight of plants and gardens . . .
They bore her lightly on the bier. Four women,
Four friends – she would have called them girls –
    stepped in

And claimed the final lift beneath the hawthorn.

Höfn

The three-tongued glacier has begun to melt.
What will we do, they ask, when boulder-milt
Comes wallowing across the delta flats

And the miles-deep shag-ice makes its move?
I saw it, ridged and rock-set, from above,
Undead grey-gristed earth-pelt, aeon-scruff,

And feared its coldness that still seemed enough
To iceblock the plane window dimmed with breath,
Deepfreeze the seep of adamantine tilth

And every warm, mouthwatering word of mouth.

Tate's Avenue

Not the brown and fawn car rug, that first one
Spread on sand by the sea but breathing land-breaths,
Its vestal folds unfolded, its comfort zone
Edged with a fringe of sepia-coloured wool tails.

Not the one scraggy with crusts and eggshells
And olive stones and cheese and salami rinds
Laid out by the torrents of the Guadalquivir
Where we got drunk before the corrida.

Instead, again, it's locked-park Sunday Belfast,
A walled back yard, the dustbins high and silent
As a page is turned, a finger twirls warm hair
And nothing gives on the rug or the ground beneath it.

I lay at my length and felt the lumpy earth,
Keen-sensed more than ever through discomfort,
But never shifted off the plaid square once.
When we moved I had your measure and you had mine.

The Blackbird of Glanmore

On the grass when I arrive,
Filling the stillness with life,
But ready to scare off
At the very first wrong move.
In the ivy when I leave.

It's you, blackbird, I love.

I park, pause, take heed.
Breathe. Just breathe and sit
And lines I once translated
Come back: 'I want away
To the house of death, to my father

Under the low clay roof.'

And I think of one gone to him,
A little stillness dancer –
Haunter-son, lost brother –
Cavorting through the yard,
So glad to see me home,

My homesick first term over.

And think of a neighbour's words
Long after the accident:
'Yon bird on the shed roof,
Up on the ridge for weeks –
I said nothing at the time

But I never liked yon bird.'

The automatic lock
Clunks shut, the blackbird's panic
Is shortlived, for a second
I've a bird's-eye view of myself,
A shadow on raked gravel

In front of my house of life.

Hedge-hop, I am absolute
For you, your ready talkback,
Your each stand-offish comeback,
Your picky, nervy goldbeak –
On the grass when I arrive,

In the ivy when I leave.

'Had I not been awake'

Had I not been awake I would have missed it,
A wind that rose and whirled until the roof
Pattered with quick leaves off the sycamore

And got me up, the whole of me a-patter,
Alive and ticking like an electric fence:
Had I not been awake I would have missed it,

It came and went so unexpectedly
And almost it seemed dangerously,
Returning like an animal to the house,

A courier blast that there and then
Lapsed ordinary. But not ever
After. And not now.

The Conway Stewart

'Medium', 14-carat nib,
Three gold bands in the clip-on screw-top,
In the mottled barrel a spatulate, thin

Pump-action lever
The shopkeeper
Demonstrated,

The nib uncapped,
Treating it to its first deep snorkel
In a newly opened ink-bottle,

Guttery, snottery,
Letting it rest then at an angle
To ingest,

Giving us time
To look together and away
From our parting, due that evening,

To my longhand
'Dear'
To them, next day.

Chanson d'Aventure

Love's mysteries in souls do grow,
But yet the body is his book.

I

Strapped on, wheeled out, forklifted, locked
In position for the drive,
Bone-shaken, bumped at speed,

The nurse a passenger in front, you ensconced
In her vacated corner seat, me flat on my back –
Our postures all the journey still the same,

Everything and nothing spoken,
Our eyebeams threaded laser-fast, no transport
Ever like it until then, in the sunlit cold

Of a Sunday morning ambulance
When we might, O my love, have quoted Donne
On love on hold, body and soul apart.

II

Apart: the very word is like a bell
That the sexton Malachy Boyle outrolled
In illo tempore in Bellaghy

Or the one I tolled in Derry in my turn
As college bellman, the haul of it there still
In the heel of my once capable

Warm hand, hand that I could not feel you lift
And lag in yours throughout that journey
When it lay flop-heavy as a bellpull

And we careered at speed through Dungloe,
Glendoan, our gaze ecstatic and bisected
By a hooked-up drip-feed to the cannula.

III

The charioteer at Delphi holds his own,
His six horses and chariot gone,
His left hand lopped

From a wrist protruding like an open spout,
Bronze reins astream in his right, his gaze ahead
Empty as the space where the team should be,

His eyes-front, straight-backed posture like my own
Doing physio in the corridor, holding up
As if once more I'd found myself in step

Between two shafts, another's hand on mine,
Each slither of the share, each stone it hit
Registered like a pulse in the timbered grips.

Miracle

Not the one who takes up his bed and walks
But the ones who have known him all along
And carry him in –

Their shoulders numb, the ache and stoop deeplocked
In their backs, the stretcher handles
Slippery with sweat. And no let-up

Until he's strapped on tight, made tiltable
And raised to the tiled roof, then lowered for healing.
Be mindful of them as they stand and wait

For the burn of the paid-out ropes to cool,
Their slight lightheadedness and incredulity
To pass, those ones who had known him all along.

Human Chain

for Terence Brown

Seeing the bags of meal passed hand to hand
In close-up by the aid workers, and soldiers
Firing over the mob, I was braced again

With a grip on two sack corners,
Two packed wads of grain I'd worked to lugs
To give me purchase, ready for the heave –

The eye-to-eye, one-two, one-two upswing
On to the trailer, then the stoop and drag and drain
Of the next lift. Nothing surpassed

That quick unburdening, backbreak's truest payback,
A letting go which will not come again.
Or it will, once. And for all.

from Route 110

for Anna Rose

I

In a stained front-buttoned shopcoat –
Sere brown piped with crimson –
Out of the Classics bay into an aisle

Smelling of dry rot and disinfectant
She emerges, absorbed in her coin-count,
Eyes front, right hand at work

In the slack marsupial vent
Of her change-pocket, thinking what to charge
For a used copy of *Aeneid* VI.

Dustbreath bestirred in the cubicle mouth
I inhaled as she slid my purchase
Into a deckle-edged brown paper bag.

Once the driver wound a little handle
The destination names began to roll
Fast-forward in their panel, and everything

Came to life. Passengers
Flocked to the kerb like agitated rooks
Around a rookery, all go

But undecided. At which point the inspector
Who ruled the roost in bus station and bus
Separated and directed everybody

By calling not the names but the route numbers,
And so we scattered as instructed, me
For Route 110, Cookstown via Toome and Magherafelt.

XII

And now the age of births. As when once
At dawn from the foot of our back garden
The last to leave came with fresh-plucked flowers

To quell whatever smells of drink and smoke
Would linger on where mother and child were due
Later that morning from the nursing home,

So now, as a thank-offering for one
Whose long wait on the shaded bank has ended,
I arrive with my bunch of stalks and silvered heads

Like tapers that won't dim
As her earthlight breaks and we gather round
Talking baby talk.

'The door was open and the house was dark'

in memory of David Hammond

The door was open and the house was dark
Wherefore I called his name, although I knew
The answer this time would be silence

That kept me standing listening while it grew
Backwards and down and out into the street
Where as I'd entered (I remember now)

The streetlamps too were out.
I felt, for the first time there and then, a stranger,
Intruder almost, wanting to take flight

Yet well aware that here there was no danger,
Only withdrawal, a not unwelcoming
Emptiness, as in a midnight hangar

On an overgrown airfield in late summer.

In the Attic

I

Like Jim Hawkins aloft in the cross-trees
Of *Hispaniola*, nothing underneath him
But still green water and clean bottom sand,

The ship aground, the canted mast far out
Above a sea-floor where striped fish pass in shoals –
And when they've passed, the face of Israel Hands

That rose in the shrouds before Jim shot him dead
Appears to rise again . . . 'But he was dead enough,'
The story says, 'being both shot and drowned.'

II

A birch tree planted twenty years ago
Comes between the Irish Sea and me
At the attic skylight, a man marooned

In his own loft, a boy
Shipshaped in the crow's nest of a life,
Airbrushed to and fro, wind-drunk, braced

By all that's thrumming up from keel to masthead,
Rubbing his eyes to believe them and this most
Buoyant, billowy, topgallant birch.

III

Ghost-footing what was then the *terra firma*
Of hallway linoleum, grandfather now appears,
His voice a-waver like the draught-prone screen

They'd set up in the Club Rooms earlier
For the matinee I've just come back from.
'And Isaac Hands,' he asks, 'Was Isaac in it?'

His memory of the name a-waver too,
His mistake perpetual, once and for all,
Like the single splash when Israel's body fell.

IV

As I age and blank on names,
As my uncertainty on stairs
Is more and more the lightheadedness

Of a cabin boy's first time on the rigging,
As the memorable bottoms out
Into the irretrievable,

It's not that I can't imagine still
That slight untoward rupture and world-tilt
As a wind freshened and the anchor weighed.

A Kite for Aibhín

after 'L'Aquilone' by Giovanni Pascoli (1855–1912)

Air from another life and time and place,
Pale blue heavenly air is supporting
A white wing beating high against the breeze,

And yes, it is a kite! As when one afternoon
All of us there trooped out
Among the briar hedges and stripped thorn,

I take my stand again, halt opposite
Anahorish Hill to scan the blue,
Back in that field to launch our long-tailed comet.

And now it hovers, tugs, veers, dives askew,
Lifts itself, goes with the wind until
It rises to loud cheers from us below.

Rises, and my hand is like a spindle
Unspooling, the kite a thin-stemmed flower
Climbing and carrying, carrying farther, higher

The longing in the breast and planted feet
And gazing face and heart of the kite flier
Until string breaks and – separate, elate –

The kite takes off, itself alone, a windfall.

In Time

for Síofra

Energy, balance, outbreak:
Listening to Bach
I saw you years from now
(More years than I'll be allowed)
Your toddler wobbles gone,
A sure and grown woman.

Your bare foot on the floor
Keeps me in step; the power
I first felt come up through
Our cement floor long ago
Palps your sole and heel
And earths you here for real.

An oratorio
Would be just the thing for you:
Energy, balance, outbreak
At play for their own sake
But for now we foot it lightly
In time, and silently.

18 August 2013

Index